WHEN THEY GO AND YOU DO NOT

A BLOG AND PLAYS ABOUT
DYING AND COMING BACK TO LIFE

When They Go and You Do Not: A Blog and Plays About
Dying and Coming Back to Life
©2011 Susan Merson

ALL RIGHTS RESERVED
No part of this book may be reproduced in any form, by photocopying or by any electronic or mechanical means, including information storage or retrieval systems, without permission in writing from both the copyright owner and the publisher of this book, except for the minimum words needed for review.

The plays, *Recognition*, *Carla Tells Us What Happened in the Blue Bedroom*, and *When They Go and You Do Not* are works of fiction. Any similarities to real places, events, or persons living or dead is coincidental or used fictitiously and not to be construed as real.

Paperback
ISBN: 978-1-935188-41-4

Edited by Janet Elaine Smith
Cover by Star Publish and Susan Merson
Interior design by Star Publish

A Star Publish LLC
[blocpress]
Publication

www.starpublishllc.com

Published in 2011
Printed in the United States of America

WHEN THEY GO AND YOU DO NOT

A BLOG AND PLAYS ABOUT
DYING AND COMING BACK TO LIFE

Susan Merson

A Star Publish LLC Book

Dedication

To those who lived, supported and loved us through this transition, well, grateful isn't big enough a word.

We all made it and we are all changed.

To our beautiful daughter, Sofia Angelique. A record of a time she knew too tenderly and too young.

And to my beautiful partner, husband and friend, Tony Shultz, who wanted this story to be told.

October 2011

TABLE OF CONTENTS

INTRODUCTION

FROM THE BEGINNING TO THE END TO THE BEGINNING
An essay of transition by Rev. Jane Stormont Galloway

WRITINGS ON TRANSITION by Susan Merson

THE BLOG:

INCH BY INCH: the journey of the prince

THE PLAYS:

RECOGNITION, a one act

CARLA TELLS US WHAT HAPPENED IN THE BLUE BEDROOM, a monologue

WHEN THEY GO AND YOU DO NOT, a solo piece

Introduction

FROM THE BEGINNING TO THE END TO THE BEGINNING
An essay of transition

From the moment we breathe our first breath we are going through one transition after another. It interests me that so many are so afraid of change, as the nature of being human is one of constant evolution.

I was in The Gap the other day and heard an infant in a double stroller crying bitterly as the mother struggled to get her baby-wrap in place to pick her up. The scene was interesting for a few reasons: one was that the baby had a sister of about 2 1/2 years old, who was playing with a computerized game dispassionately as the baby cried to the high heavens, alarming all of the shoppers in The Gap.

There was a bigger story there. I saw a dynamic which would no doubt play itself out in a million ways over the years...sibling rivalry, an overwhelmed mother, the works. But here was the interesting part to me. The second the mother picked up the baby, it stopped crying.

I mean the second...not a couple of snuffles and then some quiet.

Instant peace. I was vicariously comforted by the power of that obvious connection to Source which was, in this case, Mommy.

I recognized in that bonding scenario the feeling for which I seek in moments when I am called to transition out of the familiar—again—and to step into the unknown.

But I digress.

The question of what is different about later life transitions is one which presumes that we have all conquered the developmental stages which prepare us for the almost continual loss of later life.

If we have, we have probably endured at least one loss from which we thought we would never recover. Sometimes we don't make it. I have met women who simply stopped living after a divorce, or the death of a parent or child, spouse or beloved pet. I have studied why people sometimes just get stuck, stopped at some loss or other, and can't move on. I have learned that these are frequently the people who become hoarders. As if setting an archaeological dig in place to hold the possibility of the loss reversing, hoarders create a layer of the lost person's clothes, furniture or belongings. They keep newspapers and books and old receipts, as though perhaps the lost one will come back to claim those days or hours and want a record of life to be in place...a record of life lived while they were away. These are the people who stop, who cannot bear the pain of letting go. I have been told by a reliable authority that the largest mental health issue among seniors is hoarding.

We do not live in a society in the United States in 2011 in which getting older seems to bring a feeling of happiness. The extended family system has broken down, seemingly irreparably, the healthcare system is not geared to holistic treatment and the culture is focused on everything young. The wisdom of the elders is not sought out by the vast majority. And so the most sensitive among us sometimes choose to surround themselves with the artifacts of a more connected time. Others just lose their minds for real and go into a state of memory loss or detachment or mental illness for which we have many diagnoses. But I have a feeling we would have fewer diagnoses of dementia or idiopathic mental illness if we had greater esteem building and comforting and welcoming resources for our older citizens.

And then I have met the people I think we are interested in here. That group would include me. I think the best way to describe us is as survivors who become thrivers by being willing to go actually live through the excruciating pain of one loss or another and stay conscious.

Why do we come up against the same crises, the same agonizing losses and somehow manage to hold onto something larger than that loss?

In my own life I have shed several different versions of myself over the years. I shed the young woman who wanted more than anything to be loved when I faced the demise of my first great love. I had a choice to either go with him into a life of ashram living and guru worship or to step out alone, into my passion, which was then acting. And I chose to step out alone. I shed the young actress and the older actress and I shed the New Yorker. I shed the not-so-young woman desperate to have a child, and I grieved the loss of that dream by also shedding a very deep sense of connectedness with the husband I hoped would father that child. I shed the happy story of a passionate student returning to graduate school to stand in the truth of a sexual harassment situation at that school. I dared to defend myself and other women and our right to be safe to learn in previously male dominated professional settings and halls of higher education.

I could chronicle many of the points along the trajectory of my life in which I was faced with a similar crushing loss or seemingly catastrophic decision, but as I reflect upon them, they all are essentially the same.

They were each moments in which I was given a horrible life moment, and presented with the choice to either go with the path of seeming least resistance—whatever that was at the time—or to reconnect with the inner guidance point and inherent integrity which defines me.

Each one of those moments required a shedding of some former version of myself which felt safer than the unknown.

But the unknown became less unknown because of the earlier transitions I had lived through…to tell the tale, to see a young woman be inspired by my courage or something I could help her see. And so far…I have chosen to listen to the deeper voice, to my "gut," even when it felt so scary I could almost feel the resistance to it in my bones.

I allowed the life stages I wanted to be my story to become the life stages that really were my life. And there was loss, and more loss, and then—new gains, a new sense of mastery, of purpose, of willingness to stand in my own truth. I shed those earlier identities but I did not lose their lessons or the gifts they gave me. I am those earlier identities, but I am more than the sum of their parts. And progressively I have begun to meet the woman I really am, and to recognize her as separate from the woman I wrote the story about…the one my script wanted me to be.

I'm actually starting to like getting to know her—well, *me*.

A sense of self.

It cannot be bought, though therapy can be paid for, and probably helps a lot. It cannot be bestowed upon one by anyone else, though God knows I and many of my women friends spent years trying to find the perfect Prince Charming to do the deed. It cannot be taken away either, but that is a tricky one. Because it seems that it is always a letting go which allows us to keep ourselves. And at each moment when that is required, it feels scary all over again.

I thank God for my friends. I thank God that I know a few people who really know me and who remind me of who I am when the darkness threatens. And ultimately I thank God for God. Because that Mommy in The Gap is really a surrogate for our deeper connectedness to our Source.

On my way to Goodwill. Gotta shed some stuff. Can't wait to see what tomorrow brings.

My friend of 40 years lost her husband to Mesotheleoma.

It was a shocking and unbelievably fast loss.

It was a loss that intruded upon a complicated relationship between husband and wife who were mid-dialogue about their relationship.

And it was a loss that left Susan a widow.

I will never forget seeing her at the funeral as we saw Tony for the last time. Who was she now?

Susan was consumed with grief.

She shrugged her shoulders at me as my husband and I filed by Tony's casket, as if to say, "Look at this! How did this happen? How did this become my life suddenly?"

And then at the reception following the funeral I saw the resilience which I knew to be the essence of my friend.

I was having a conversation with our mutual friend who told me that her plastic surgeon was having a sale on a procedure both Susan and I were interested in.

Suddenly the grieving widow—my friend Susan—jumped into the middle of our conversation and said, "Yes, Janie, Dr. B. is having a sale! You have to check it out!!"

And I knew my friend would find her way back.

These plays are representative of her way back, and through, and into to a new normal.

I lived some of this with her. I watched her tackle the forces that were trying to pull her into despair, and triumph over them.

And now you will be the recipient of some of the lessons of that journey back.

These are magnificent pieces, and they are made even better by the fact that they are art made from the ashes of a life...used as the foundation for the next life.

You will be changed in the best way possible as you read them.

Rev. Dr. Jane Stormont Galloway
Mandala / H"artWorks

Journey/Wholeness/Artistic Expression/Integrative Healing

Rev. Dr. Jane Stormont Galloway, Founder/Pastor, Mandala Center for Conscious Living, Founder/Executive Director, H'artWorks, Inc., has long been passionate about healing the communities around her. She is a 30-year career actor, educator, and counselor with a specialty in addictions recovery and therapeutic theatre. She's a community builder/activist who focuses on social justice concerns, including AIDS treatment and support services, mental health and holistic healing for all ages and abilities. Ordained in the AME Church, she is now a minister in the United Church of Christ, and has both Master's and Doctoral degrees from Claremont School of Theology.

In October of 2000, Rev. Dr. Jane founded Immanuel Center for Conscious Living in Long Beach, an Ancient Wisdom/New Thought congregation affiliated with the United Church of Christ and is also working in collaboration with Agape International Spiritual Center. Immanuel is a transcultural, open and affirming spiritual center, with a focus on social justice and on using the Arts, Spiritual Practice and Selfless service to open people to their inner magnificence. In 2001, Dr. Galloway founded H'artWorks, a 501 (c) 3 Arts and Education nonprofit which serves the students of HoraceMann Elementary School—a Title One School—and other youth who would not otherwise experience excellence in arts training. She has succeeded in creating a neighborhood center focused on providing a "home away from home" where youth have access to technology, arts, job training and mentoring in a safe, supportive environment.

Dr. Galloway's vision for the community of Long Beach is larger than her passion for the arts, greater than her devotion to the mentally ill and differently-abled, wider than her dedication to addictions recovery. Her vision for Long Beach is to empower it to become the model by which the rest of the country, and world, will follow—a model for peace amidst diversity.

She has focused unflinchingly on encouraging open communication among the many groups in this "most multicultural city in the United States," and beyond. It is Dr. Galloway's emphatic belief that by focusing on the commonality of humanity, while honoring the individuality, Long Beach will be successful in establishing a Beloved Community where diversity is embraced and celebrated, and not the source of division and destruction.

INCH BY INCH:
the journey of the prince
a blog

DECEMBER 28, 2007
HELLO AND GOODBYE

Hope this finds everyone well and readying themselves for the new year.

We are facing a new challenge in our family and we wanted to let you know about it now though our information is basic. Sorry that we have to do this via email, but phone calls are a bit difficult at this point.

Tony had been experiencing some difficult breathing and health problems in the last few weeks, though the heart arrhythmia problem has always been the thing that we thought would be of most concern.

We were very surprised to learn that he had developed fluid on his lungs which was initially identified as pneumonia about ten days ago. The fluid was drained and no bad elements were found but we proceeded to biopsy because a CT scan showed a background akin to Van Gogh's *Starry, Starry Night*—

We were also surprised and distressed to find yesterday after the major lung biopsy that his right lung is full of cancerous tumor. Actually the quote from the thoracic surgeon is "sheets and sheets of tumor."

We know very little more at this point in terms of prognosis or treatment.

Today we have a confirmed diagnosis of Mesothelioma—the asbestos cancer—usually the gift to construction workers or Steve McQueen clones; but now confirmed as filling the right lung of my handsome husband. Go know—

So, he is now resting and healing from the biopsy and should be home from the hospital by Monday or Tuesday. We will meet with the oncologist on Thursday and then we will begin to get more of an idea.

Mostly, Tony wanted you to know he is fine, clear eyed and seeing every and all parts of the equation and we are taking everything exactly one moment at a time.

Please feel free to tell whoever might need to know. Tony is clear about that, too.

I won't be answering the phone too much in the next few days, but email is always good.

We are surrounded by lots of loving friends and very smart doctors and now we need some prayers.

Hope to be in touch with everyone soon. Once he heals from this surgery, visits probably welcome. To be continued and much love from us to you.

JANUARY 3, 2008
HERE IS WHAT WE KNOW TODAY

Thanks are just a part of what everyone in our full and lusciously endowed community deserves. Just know how important that love and light stuff really is—

The beauty and support of every shoulder and every sigh does really ease the load, so count on me when your time comes—because we know these times come to us all, one after the other.

And here is where we are today. Mostly Tony and Sofie and I are solid and strong, enjoying the true weirdness of living and its violent perfection.

T and I went to the doctor today. The oncology center to the stars complete with cappuccino and cocoa makers. Felt like *Willy Wonka and the Chocolate Factory* with a great deal of living happening in every corner. They strike just the right note, but we won't be spending much time there.

The cancer is now clearly in Tony's left lung as well as the right. The liquid excreted night before last in the ER was indeed pleural liquid giving us a preview of this fact. Options were limited to us.

Surgery, awful and not an option since it is spread. Chemo would extend his life perhaps a month or two at best—and those months full of poison pumping and hours in a clinic with IV's and phosphoresence—" Why rake muck", as Buber says, "when we can be stringing pearls to the delight of heaven?"

Bottom line is. Anywhere from 6 months to a year at the outside if we are lucky.

At this point and this may change of course—Tony has decided that, after the fabulous Evelyn model, he would rather live his life than run after it. He wants to feel good and celebrate with friends and family and take care of business and have the joy of all that until that doesn't work, and then we will have hospice here at home and all usher him over. I am fully in support of this decision—we all feel good about it.

There is no cancer warrior game to play, We have other things to do with the time we have. Fighting for fight sake gives very little return. Please understand that. We are not in the pep talk realm. The CT scan was immensely clear that there is nothing to "go for"—except beauty and joy and time together.

So we are going to celebrate and enjoy each other and laugh and cry and drink champagne for now and do what we can, and then when soup and low voices are in order we will do that too.

We love and value each and every one of you. We look forward to your support. Email remains the best still but things will have an odd normalcy now and evenings are good to come by for now. We will just play it as we go. Do check in by email if you'd like.

Sofie is fabulous and clear and she says she'll be around until we all make her sick and then she'll head out to be with friends.

We came home and all sat together and talked it all through together and then had a good lunch at the Grand Luxe and T had a huge chocolate shake and fries, fuck it, and tonight Sof and T will watch some football together and hang with whoever comes by.

So we are good and we are strong and we are full of life and living and we know you are too. Feel free to pass this info around.

And we hope to see you or talk to you when we can. Me, being the curmudgeon I am and T, enjoying the fruits of his life—your friendship and love and support to the next months of adventure.

Sofie needs to get school work done and we all have jobs to do.
Much, much love

4 AM THURSDAY THE 9TH OF JAN, 2008
REPORTING IN

Since Thursday we have been
1: drinking and eating an enormous amount
2: laughing raucously and fully
3: appreciating the fine tuned madness of excellent scotch
4: doing dishes and washing floors
5: talking too much and sleeping too little
6: feeling good and right about our decision to opt for quality of life,

Tony is
1: handsome, elegant, centered
2: taking care of business, attending to details, working as much as he can and

3: driving his excellent Audi and wearing his elegant brown cashmere coat
4: having massage
5: squeezing my hand when requested.
6: feeling pretty good and
7: just yesterday started feeling a little tired

Medically, we are—
1: coordinating doctors and seeing another maven surgeon at UCLA who has dealt with Mesothelioma exclusively for many years
2: researching clinical trials that might extend life without impairing quality of life
(Though frankly I am feeling that may just be prolonging the agony- go know)
3: getting too many cooks in the pot and finding it a challenge to leave too many fucking messages on too many phone lines and all that jazz.

Business wise—
1:Tony is getting all his business stuff handled
2:We are meeting with appropriate folk about all the stuff
3:I am filing too many papers in too big a notebook with too many details

I am trying to sort thru legal issues and marveling at the sleaze factor of "foundation" sites that set themselves up as purveyors of medical information and then turn out to be fronts created by law firms who are courting victims of the disease as possible litigants against the manufacturers of asbestos products. Money talks, kids oh you betcha. Sure I want some, but oh you kid, a real nausea factor there. To be continued.

Sofie is
1: fabulous
2: back at school and getting the work done
3: getting the support she needs
4: being pretty magnificent in all ways

You are
1: being wonderfully supportive, cooking too much food,
2: seeking "occupations" that will relieve the itchy horror of this inevitable terrible journey for yourselves and us
3: sending us love and light and information and care and bad jokes
4: being just exactly perfect in your perfectness and friendship and respect of history and your own journeys in connection with our own histories. This journey is everyone's. It connects with our own personal searing slashes of life—everybody has those—and in going thru this with us everyone steps a bit closer to healing their own pain.

You can
1: read this blog and stay tuned
2: know that you are on the list for counsel, food, help when we need it
3: stay connected with love

We will probably go to a weekend celebratory mode next week. During the week we'll keep it low key and keep the place as sane as possible for homework and rest and small events and on the weekends we'll go to an open house thing where everyone who wants to can come by and eat and act inappropriately and laugh and talk and all that. We will do that as long as that makes sense and then we will do the next thing.

THIS WEEKEND
1: we are family-ed in with sister Cindy in town, so stay tuned for more info.
2: I will try to post as often as I can.

There we have it.

IN THE INTEREST OF EASE AND DELIGHT

So, in the interest of ease and delight, I pass along to you, courtesy of the fabulous Uncle Andy, courtesy of YouTube, the following meditation which I highly recommend for all of us.

http://www.youtube.com/watch?v=8p3lPw3LmKQ

Lovely niece, Hannah and Tony's newly skinn-ily and even more fabulous sister Cindy have been with us all weekend. Cindy filed some horrid papers for us.

I have hired an assistant for the duration.

Had a long sleep 'til 7 AM. Tony Shultz is watching the game, snoozing all day today until a family gathering at 4. We see the lawyer on Monday morning and I am getting even more nauseous at the research we are starting to see on some of the contaminants in glazes etc. in ceramics studios in the late 60's now to determine if that glaze was in that studio at that time.

Ah, click the link.
It's Saturday. A day of rest.
xxoo
s

SUNDAY JANUARY 13, 2008
SO WHAT CAN YOU BE AFRAID OF, LET US COUNT THE WAYS

Okay, another chink lower into the reality. A little slip lower, closer to the pit of knowing.

10 PM, Saturday night, sitting on the couch, watching the news, that was the moment.

We hit the ground running tomorrow, head to our first legal appointment and revisit the oncologist. Are there clinical trials?

Hope, let's see what is hope. What is worthy of hope? What is grace, fighting, acceptance, joy…? Wow—there's a clinic in the Bahamas, we could get a house and all hang at the beach, yeah! Or maybe, Vancouver? It's rainy this time of year... hmmm

Indigestion of the soul.

So—we looked at each other last night and we figured it out. We were really afraid. We both knew. We were shy around it. Like maybe we shouldn't let it know we knew it was with us—fear. But then, what have we got to lose anyway- so T says to me:

"I'm afraid, Susie. Are you afraid?"
"Yes, are you afraid?"
"Yep."
Silence.
"I just said I was afraid"
Beat. Beat.
"Oh, right. Sorry."
"So, what are we afraid of, do we know?" says T, just-the-facts man
"Yep, I have a really long list—" and I listed at least 27 things, and maybe then more.
It was a clattery rattle in our little living room and T said:
"Wow, you have a really long list. Mine is shorter."
"But you're scared-er, right?" I said
"Right."
Hmmm. We looked around and see if fear heard and then said fuck it. Who cares. No news there.
"Okay, let's go to bed, okay?" says T.
"Okay," I said.

And we did and we were still scared and we still slept thru the night and we still woke up and now it is a beautiful Sunday morning and I have a headache, and Sofie has gone off to pals, and Tony is watching football with his sister, and Hannah is cleaning the kitchen.
And we're still afraid.
And we're still here.
And so are you.
And it's all okay.
Talk to you tomorrow.

MONDAY JANUARY 14, 2008
STAY TUNED

Stay tuned! The waters are changing, the crystal ball is fogging up and shrieking so deeply insecure because it has no fucking idea what to predict. What's a fortune teller to do???

Ah yes, fellow travelers we have a new wrinkle to predict a new possibility from old news and who knows what the answer might be....the SHADOW Doooooooooooo....

More when there is more. Right now, clouds and sunshine and umbrellas and fog, and sweet lawyers with baby faces this morning, and dour faces of sweet doctors with new possibilities and "jump down turn around picka bale of cotton, jump down turn around picka bale of hay"— Harry Belafonte sang that one.

But we're still here—we're still here—isn't that a Stritch line??????

Oh, and we're all fighting today. He hates me, and I hate them, and She hates us both, and we're still here!!!! We're still here!!!!!

Hang onto your hats, we're in for a bumpy night!
For a year or two?

Oh, and T wants to know, if he hangs around for an extra twelve months, will he still get all those great cartons of Starbucks Java Chip everybody has been showering him with??
Always a consideration, you know.

TUESDAY, JANUARY 15, 2008
SO, A PARADIGM SHIFT FOR US.

Hello friends,
A busy day for us...errands and lunch at the Bel Air hotel for T and me being super Mom and both of us ending the day with massage and warm thoughts.

Yesterday was a big day. We met with the lawyer about a possible claim against possible asbestos exposure manufacturers. The lawyer is this sweet faced killer (I hope) who has a brother who is a lighting designer. He's a nice Yiddisha boy a little too nice for his job but T felt good about him I think and we signed on the dotted line. Then Tony got to tell his WHOLE work history as a stage technician and despite the fact that these experiences are killing him it was an enjoyable exercise for both of us, for T to remember all those theatres and light cables and catwalks and girls, and flats and hammers and painting jobs and girls and ceramic studios and culpable glazes and airplane parts and yes, of course, girls.

So, we now leave it to the lawyer to see if he can make any official connections and the only thing T has to do is a deposition in the future and either it will work or not but that's done.

Then, on the medical front we had a hell of a roller coaster day with everything from a possibility of many years, to the possibility of being a "pulmonary cripple," to the possibility of dying in two months to where I think we have landed which is probably, that:

There is indeed a confirmation of cancer in the left lung. Therefore, we will not do a biopsy there to see if it could maybe be inflammation—fantasy island surgeon stuff—that the surgeon was hoping would allow T to consider a horrendous surgery where they remove the entire right lung, the lining, the Pericardium (that's the lining of the heart) and then maybe—just maybe, if you live thru the operation, just about the time you recover from surgery you're dead from exhaustion or worse...Soooooo, frankly, I am very pleased that that is off the table.

And now so we revisit chemo and we are now being told that it might even give T another complete year so okay— they have lots of nausea drugs, and I think I can convince him to go Jacques Brel with a black beret and it may even get him to Sofie's graduation!! So hell—we're going for that.

Soooo, a couple more tortuous meetings about possible scenarios and then I think he will start the standard Cisplatin and Alimta chemo thing and we will see how it goes—

SO WE ARE NOW IN THE PARADIGM SHIFT FROM DYING FROM CANCER TO LIVING WITH CANCER (READ VOLDEMORT) BUT THIS ONE TO BE NAMED AND FACED

So, that means, sharpen your pencils and get out the cookbooks because we got a hell of a year to be living thru and we are available for social occasions, weekends in the country, dinners, lunches, brunches, football, snoozes, beach breakfasts and other quality celebrations of all kinds including periodic weeping and massages and pots of soup and volunteering to do the dishes.

Who knows how it will go, but here we are and there we'll be…with your help and love and support from which we are already eternally altered for the better.

Blessings all.
Stay tuned
Love

WEDNESDAY, JANUARY 16, 2008
LIVING IN DARFUR

So, okay then, lovely dinner last night.

We get home, climb into bed, I'm feeling a little not so sure about my stomach and in the middle of the night the flying monkeys of the fearsome flu visit and I crawl out of my conjugal bed and away from my sweet husband to the office where I can ache in peace and roll around with fluish Jewish detail and wave at T thru the window when I awake in quarantine and not wanting to breathe in his direction and then read my email with an update on almost relative Ed Ethridge, who out of nowhere is struggling with a massive heart attack stroke thing that came from the same fucking flying monkeys dive bombing just for fun…..

and then

I call my big sister for comfort and a little "oh poor baby" and then I hear that my big brother was in the hospital this week with a detached retina and nobody would call me 'cause I'm the suffering spouse person and I'm thinking this is what it must be to be a person in Darfur where all you need is a little firewood to warm up the gruel and instead you get whacked by the crazy tribal madmen when you dare to venture out into life.

Phew.

So, man oh man—everybody has it. And the only way we get thru it is to share it and shake our heads and keep on keeping on.

I thought of this as the vitamin drip I summoned to cure me dripped into my veins and my husband was at home in bed and my brother was recovering from the hospital and my almost relative Ed is struggling in the ICU and it was my Mom's 89th birthday just yesterday—which she missed because she passed over in August. Peaceful but too scared.

And tonight George Bush said it was okay official policy to keep pumping sonar into the waves to disorient the whales and dolphins and NPR featured that story on the UFO coming down for a look.

Wow. Congratulations on being on the planet right now, we've got a whole lot of keeping on to be keeping track of.
much love

THURSDAY JANUARY 17, 2008
THE RESPITE

So, my gorgeous husband stretched out on sofa like the handsome cat he is, raises his arms above his head for an extra inch of air—ah! And we talk—easy—settling into a little normal rhythm before the next storm.

I'm still recovering from flu and am cozy in pajamas not breathing in his heavily Maitake mushroomed vicinity and we just talk—like normal people after dinner, dishes in the sink, cat meowing and dog in a dream.

So, he's all healed from the biopsy. He is well now, energy full-ish, working every day reveling in all the laudatory tributes from pals far and near and I say,
"So, what do you want to do now? The next year, if we get it," I say, "What shall we do?"
So he says:
>"Friends. That's what we do. Like the day we first got the diagnosis and we were walking on Wilshire Blvd dazed and thinking about death. That's when I got it.
>
>I can't go walking around thinking about death. All these guys on the street, they're not thinking about death, they're living their lives. So that's what we're gonna do. I'm going to go to work and eat great food and lots of ice cream and do as many gatherings as I possibly can. No dreamy weekends isolating in the woods (he looks at me, the isolate, desperate for silence and solitude—okay, okay)—no weekends on lonely islands or quiet walks in Ojai. Nope, I want to be with friends and see my life."

So, it's the quiet now before the next bump. We are stretching like lazy cats and waiting for the next thing but for now we are here and there and everywhere. Gospel at the temple tomorrow, football on Sunday,

Saturday is open if anyone wants to play (!) So is Monday. I'm exhausted and cranky and he's having a great time. What else is new?

Tuesday we see the big fancy surgical oncologist, the maven in this disease, and then we make the decision to get to that chemo or this, and see how that goes.

Meantime, how are you doing? Life is good. Feel free to e Tony or give him a call.
Love is all.

HOW DID IT HAPPEN?

"The past is always carried into the present by small things. So a lily is bent by its permanence."—Michael Ondaatje

More Tuesday probably when we see the surgical oncologist. Meantime. it's late. We're snoozing. Hope you are too.

SUNDAY, JANUARY 20, 2008

Tony is anxious for Tuesday, when we will meet with Robert Cameron the big shot at UCLA. He is mostly a surgeon but he knows a lot about this stuff.

Check out the website Pacific Heart and Lung Institute for some absolutely amazing photographs of these kind of tumors being removed and the long sheath of tissue that is the tumor itself. That is only if prurient interest in all this stuff is of interest to you. It's pretty fascinating actually if you remove the fact that it's you or your beloved who is being peeled like a grape from the inside.

Breathing is being appreciated a bit more as it's getting difficult from time to time—oxygen tanks are dotting the landscape tonight. Not sure if it's the cancer or the congestive heart failure from the Atrial fib, which has been pretty much unchecked for over a year. And we have no viable cardiologist who actually calls us back, so we are so grateful to the menschy oncologist who actually calls back within a few minutes and offers clear, wise and simple advice.

So, we love Lasix and pray for lots of liquid moving out of the body.

Not much to do except wait for the surgeon, start the chemo when we can, if we can and so it goes.

Up to this point he has felt well so this marks a bit of a change but he may be just fine again tomorrow. The details of the survival months start to become more apparent to us and we are striving for balance as we make decisions about what is best, when we seek what aid, what we balance and tough out, which part of the house we keep as a cancer free zone, if any, and easy stuff like that.

I gotta go.
Love

MONDAY, JANUARY 21, 2008
I'M NOT A DOCTOR BUT I'VE PLAYED ONE ON TV.

...and it came in handy last night as the Atrial fib/flutter/heart rate gallop sent T breathless to the ER (once again) with fluid on the lung—(right one again/the one that was talc-ed).Congestive heart failure—sounds very dramatic but we've been thru this scenario a few times already. We should take a suite.

Speaking to the fairly hip nurse, we found out that Liz Taylor does have her own suite here at Cedars. It has a lovely sitting room, hardwood floors and a very nice bathroom according to our sources. Also a sitting area with a fold-out couch which sure would have come in handy last night when we both stretched out on his bed, pretending to ignore the beeps and whistles and soundtrack of all night hospital life.

He pee-ed out two and 1/4 of those ample little thermos bottle things and he was admitted and now rests (yeah, right) captive in the north tower until they can get his heart rate under 100 again so he can breathe, and then move and then head to the cancer surgeon and then figure out what the next thing is. Ah life and its unravelings...

So, once the hip nurse went home about midnight, the second neurasthenic gal, all bleached blond and square eye-glassy comes in around 1:30 AM and says:

"Oooh, so I see you have Mesothelioma. I just love to learn about new things. Like, I Googled it, but it didn't come up with anything except maybe from asbestos, so did you do asbestos? I mean how'd you get it, like what's it like?"

I raise my slack jawed head from the bed where it was trying to sleep, eyes glazed ready to strike when the gracious Mr. T begins nicely explaining to her the ins and outs of his Voldemort foe. And I try to give her the high sign by saying:

"Well, maybe it doesn't bear a great deal of conversation at the moment... (beaming "cause it's gonna kill him, asshole") but she says,

"Oh yeah. Right. I guess it's over, huh?" and then turns pertly and exits stage left.

Who is writing for ER these days, House, maybe? We want credit for that little interchange.

I guess she thought about it a little 'cause she returned a few minutes later with some injectable drug, saying:

"Ooh, hope I didn't offend you. I just think all these diseases are so cool and we don't see a lot of that stuff. Mostly not working guys around here, y'know, but I hope you're cool."

And T, to his credit, said something like:
"Well, I may not be the best educational resource for you because the fucker is killing me at moment."

She exits.

Words fail us.

"Well I guess I'll read about this one on the blog," he says.
And we collapse in laughter.

By the way, the view from his room over the hills at bout 5 AM—when the sun is just beginning to peak—is actually very beautiful. He's sleeping and I'm going home to do the same.
xxoo

TUESDAY JANUARY 22, 2008
NO ANSWERS. LOTS OF QUESTIONS

Big day today. T home from Cedars at noon. Quick run down, heart rate in better control but who knows for how long?

Little confidence in cardiologist, good meeting with surgeon at UCLA, still digesting info and will get back with details. Surgery may be an option but we will not know until mid February. They have to reanalyze some slides to see how voracious the cancer cells are, then, we need to see if the left lung is inflammation and not cancer as there continues to be a question—oncologist says cancer; thoracic surgeons say it may be inflammation Pet/CT scan will give us more info—but can't do 'til Feb 2. Need to do more blood tests and some reexamination. No answers. Lots of questions.

If surgery is an option, and we won't know 'til mid Feb then—the surgery is to remove tumor around right lung and NOT the lung itself. Pleurectomy and Decortification—then recovery, then radiation, then interferon (not covered by insurance) and disease is then treated as a chronic disorder to be managed a la diabetes /high blood pressure—(with a tired Mr. Tony and living a bit pared down financially—but I might be able to up my teaching).

This is new medical idea—not previously offered. This guy doesn't think chemo is an option—only works 40% of time on this cancer. Atrial fib is a big problem in the first week after surgery, and then of course we already have this problem but Cameron seems to think it is manageable...but we would have to talk to more cardiologists at UCLA.

So we are still digesting. The place was all razors and tongs, rock walls and fluorescent lights. Kept us waiting from 4:30-7:30, grueling, took a break to a surreal Indian restaurant with Indian MTV playing silently over my shoulder and the ghost of lunchers swallowing all the oxygen but then we got this possibility,

Surgery offers about 6 months of recovery and radiation and then perhaps chemo or not depending on what they see when they go in then an average of 18-36 months on average survival rate as opposed to a 9 month survival rate with or without chemo, this from UCLA maven surgeon.

We are digesting and gathering info.
Nothing is simple.
Nothing is decided.
Nothing is easy.

I must prepare for school and work tomorrow and please understand if I am not in touch immediately, There is a great deal to manage.
Much love to you all.

A DELIGHTFUL DIVERSION

GUESS WHAT? Even with T so sick and us so crazed, we get a little gift now and then....
...and maybe next year T and I will write THE YEAR OF LIVING CANCEROUSLY and go on the road together!

My god, how absurd is this life.

xxoo

WASHING DISHES AND DOING ORDINARY THINGS

Our friend, Vicki just said—about how surreal it all is-and then "we still have to wash dishes and do ordinary things"

And so we do. At 4:27 AM, the rains gushed from Noah's arc onto our back garden, and the sprinklers went on at the very same time, and all I could think of was all that multiplying and drowning of things, and that was not productive.

The cat meowed, agreeing, and sent me back to sleep and then the heavens roared again and it was time to drive. So, to school and then the guy at the gas station scowled at me for needing a quart of oil in the rain. Right. I get that.

And then T took a shower and T told me about his bad dreams and I put the dishes away from the dishwasher, and then we talked about whether he was going to live or die with a major incision in his body or unscathed, and then I did the email and ate a bowl of cereal and then we went to the lawyer who I yelled at because she actually was trying to be nice and do her job and then we got in the car and I didn't apologize and I came home and thought, well now that T won't be around just who gets to decide when to unplug me at the last moment?

And then I folded the laundry and posted work for my students and ate three scones and a huge plate of chicken and a mound of last night Nava's vegetables and then I talked to the other lawyer about just who and where and what and how much and how dare they and isn't it too bad that...and then I brought the garbage cans from the street.

I did put some real wood over some real mud today though and that felt real good, like I was accomplishing something.

Spoke to the menschy doctor tonight and he wished me a good weekend and it made me smile because he really meant it and I appreciated that.

SUNDAY JANUARY 27, 2008
SO LET US GATHER OUR GREAT HEARTS AND MINDS
GENERIC DISCLAIMER: THE FOLLOWING IS RUMINATIVE IN NATURE. NO NEED TO BURDEN YOURSELF IF YOU JUST WANT AN UPDATE. THAT'S AT THE VERY END.

There are no mistakes.

"Life is right in any case" said Rainer Maria Rilke in Letters to A Young Poet.
Well, perhaps life is right as it holds the inexorable and we here are placed within it to be silent in the roar and try to ride the wave. The WAY we

ride the wave, the tools we bring to bear, the place we may be in our own journey of discovery is surely varied—some do better worse or draw—no credit to be given or taken—just the way it is.

Still with the "rightness "of life there is this claw, the terrible streak of raw tissue exposed as one moves through life's certainties—birth, death, gain, loss, losing.

The idea of our God and energetic governance has certainly evolved as we have evolved. We were privileged to be at Disney Hall the other night to witness the Britten War Requiem—(in fabulous seats with even more fabulous company, by the way, so many thanks).

This is the thought:—the punishing God, damning souls to eternal death for dying as combatants of lousy war, the idea of God the King, sitting on high, slamming his zap gun thru the exposed guts of penitents. THAT God, we extol thee, beg mercy from thee, THAT God—that is the God of a time needing to be kept in line! A time when everyone better – goddam— live on the straight and narrow! Keeping the earthlings separate from the Gods! God has pee-ed his territory. We are not invited, except on our knees—but That God—can't possibly address our time, can He?

Okay—waiting now for a thunderbolt, seems to be fine, so will continue.

My point here is that T's illness, the recent news that two other good friends from the east have been diagnosed with strokes or cancer, the more recent news that the exalted and vibrant Chris Allport has been swept away in an avalanche—yes signs and wonders—in Wrightwood—Big Bear—omigod- this week one year almost exactly after mentor and friend Curt D decided to end his life, the warming of the planet, the rains, the snow drifts, the loss of life-long occupations, the visiting UFOs (two reports in last week), the exhortation from our leaders that we can save our souls and the economy by shopping...yes, by shopping....asks us to consider—please consider "the elements doth contend about us"—all of us.

We have energetic matters of the planet being brought to bear, bringing

their considerable forces upon our rather human backs, and how do we meet these forces? With acceptance? Defiance? Elevation, surely. Meditation, some say. Vitamin shakes?
Do we meet the day as penitents groveling on our knees in front of the great Oz? Do we stand as victims at Babi Yar and wait for the bullet in our brains that will neatly collapse us into the graves we have conveniently dug ourselves? Or do we attempt to understand that we are part of the great Oz—we are part and parcel of the great creative Oz that is part and parcel of the whole shebang, and how do we meet this? How do we prepare? How do we listen? How do we bend and not break?

I don't think sit-ups will do the trick. There is a larger, more central call from the universe that is hooking us on a cellular level and no longer asking but telling us to expand, expand, expand now to try to get a handle or at least run the rapid without losing too many limbs.

Oy vey. Can a Jewish girl from the Midwest possibly reach the mountaintop and manage the Promised Land? Only if one stands atop the hill raises ones arms to the sky and believes the winds will raise her upward perhaps.

I wonder if I have lost you all, "madness and despair has descended on Citrus—poor thing" say you all. No, not really. Certainly not.

It's just that there is more here at stake than our little lives and enormous loves—are we meant to take to heart the placard GOD IS LOVE— plastered against the church wall? Is GOD'S LOVE enough? What is it for God's sake? Who is it? Is it us, and are we up to the task of integration into the cosmos? Both in this life and out of it?

Here is where humility and grace come in. Lots of the first and prayers for the second.

Hope you were able to follow all that...

Sunday morning "complacencies of the boudoir"—as Wallace Stephens might say.

T goes to the basketball game today with cool cousin, Sofie dines with excellent soul guide. I find hands to rub my body. Tomorrow we meet with oncologist for more opinions and so it goes.

Much love.

TUESDAY, JANUARY 29, 2008
BARGAINING

So, if I shake my head and say no, walk away from the table and refuse the best offer, will the guy call me back and give me a better deal?

On our honeymoon in Morocco, lo these many hippie years ago, we walked the Souk in Marrakesh, and amber beads caught my eye. Thick, I thought, and so rich and my husband adept at negotiation even then—pre real estate life—tossed out 5 dinar (or whatever the Moroccan currency was) and the grinning merchant sensing the hook in the cheek says ah sir, but surely—15 dinar is a better price and we turned away with a smile knowing we were hooked but choosing to believe we had power and began to walk away…and the merchant called after us—
"Ah sir, sir, 15 dinar no good for you, 5 dinar no good for me, so what will be goodness" he said, toothy and rotten.

I believe there was even sweet tea in aluminum pressed tin pots and mint leaves caught between his black teeth and we did indeed settle midway. A magnificent 9 rupiah winning the prize. I took my amber beads and wore them proudly until that evening when Tony, unable to leave well enough alone, took the tell tale match from the bug ridden hotel lobby and placed its blue flame under the bead.
"True amber doesn't blacken," he said.
But my plastic beads did. I still wore them. I had them, we bought them and I wore them not really seeing them as a symbol of deception but rather as a emblem of making life work—going with the negotiation, accepting the prize, making lemonade from lemons and "making magic" from scorn, as my mother once said.

So, we are in the dickering mode with god and oncologists, and T trying to pin down just exactly what he will get from this deal or that being offered by the gods.

There was another negotiation in Morocco. I swapped two pairs of jeans with monkey merchants to secure him a geode. I thought he would be so happy that I was so brave to meet the monkey merchants alone and make the deal without him. And he was furious. I had given away his best jeans to the scummy scam artists at the edge of the town of lamb chops and Shit Mountain. So, I learned not to bargain without him and instead I watch from the sidelines and finger the geodes I already have and count them lucky enough for they are in our hands and we have not been raped and brutalized by the monkey merchants,
quite yet.

I will see where he will land.

We still have no answers, the bargaining with fate and PET scans is falsely empowering perhaps, but it has drawn me from my bed at 3 am and I am dickering for dawn.

THURSDSAY, JANUARY 31, 2008
OH FRABJOUS DAY

Oh frabjous day,calloo callay…
Night before last the dread Voldemort started squirming again in my loved ones breast—a squeak, then a gurgle, a wheeze like a treacherous barn door flapping before the cyclone.

So, brilliant folk we are, hoping to avoid the dark dawn visits to the asshole nurse at Cedars ER once again, we call the cardiologist, get him out of surgery and insist that he see Tin the afternoon before the symptoms grow and mutate and metastasize as a few other things seem to be doing. So, T hauls himself to Bev Hills in his Jag and greying beard, hangs his cashmere coat against the table and with a sigh he lies on the slab to be hooked and slathered.
"Toorn on ze elektrodeszzzz, Herr Profezzor!"

And the small white tape unfurls its Slytherin tongue from the EKG box and there is a beep…beep..beep…beep…beep… and again beep…beep…beep…beep. Steady, consistent, miraculously straight forward, simple, lacking pernicious inconsistency.

For the first time in SEVEN years, the little tape and the steady beep signal a heart rate in sinus, absolutely steady, in rhythm, no ragtime Bossa Nova beats, and no moment of suspense, wondering if the heart will beat again. Nope. The miracle of steady expectation—present in the heart of my handsome prince.

And the doctor looks at T and T, he—and they tiptoe, mystified from their respective cloaks and down the hall and out the door, back to their own lives for there is joy in Mudville because the clamor has calmed. Who knows why? Maybe Eun, the cutie pie acupuncturist's, rotten prune juice tea? Maybe the simple resolve of no running and lots of being in the moment. Who knows? But the heart is steady and strong and clear and so we have that. Hmmm.

And today T picked up a big check and tossed it in the bank and took advantage of our fabulous Pleasure Account at the Four Seasons (oh so many thanks you's for that fabulous respite of luxurious overkill) and returned home to spaghetti sauce and scotch and tales of Sofie's finals and analysis of her educators complete with n depth analysis, sound effects and laughter.

All in all not a bad day…taking it one inch, one day at a time.

We know more Tuesday.

Last week, T, out of the generosity of spirit, spent too much time hearing tales of cancer and cures, and clinical trials and calls to battle and all the stuff I refuse to let in my sphere. It is exhausting. Sh-h-h-h-h-h. Hold your counsel, dear friends, trust we are connected and clear, and doing what needs to be done. Let us look to the wisdom of his heart and the wonderful sign that used to grace the entrance to the transcendent grounds of Wheelers Hot Springs in Ojai and let us all "slow right down."

And let us say, amen.

TUESDAY, FEBRUARY 5, 2008
AH SILENCE

The joy of nothing special has graced us for the last few days. Super bowl parties, and corny school silent auctions, and dinner with friends, and talks of Obama and Hillary, and watching the Mexican plumbers break their backs dig dig digging the trench to our new gorgeous garden bathroom. The important stuff.

Tony has been quoted as saying he's had more fun in the last month than he's had in years. Scotch and chocolate and friends and hilarity and naps on the couch…well you get the picture but. oh well, the jig is up or almost up. So now to the difficult decisions with no answers, too many opinions and no real out except through the miserable center.

I tell you—this staying in the moment thing is the best case, but this moment—this morning gave us the results of the latest pet/ct scan.

On the one hand—as one Jew once said—the left lung has NO inflammation and so as of this moment, the thoracic surgeons were right and the left lung was inflammation and not cancer. Okay, that's good.

But, the right lung, oh…now there's a new and different story. More growth, more mass, more enlarged Lymphnodes though no official trace of cancer according to pet scan in lymph system yet. Soooo, the time to act is now, surgery or chemo or nothing.

We have ruled out nothing. So—surgery or chemo. Difficult choice since the options offered are still unclear. We go back to surgeon on Friday and wait another three hours. Bringing Scrabble this time, and see what kind of cells are predominant in biopsy slide.
…and blah, blah, blah.

We have no answers and more dread. Fuck eloquence.

WEDNESDAY, FEBRUARY 6, 2008
ON BEING A JEW

One wonders over the years of Hebrew school and chicken soup just who cares where you come from. I mean each culture has its virtues, but I have learned slowly, hard-ly, that being a Jew is just who I am. It has no particular virtue except to have formed me somehow. Many in my camp snickered when they heard I was marrying a Tony from California. Nobody was so sure about him. Too cute, too hip, and with a heart like that? And those eyes? And he sang???? Goyishe coup, they snickered, those aunts of mine, and the Jewish boyfriends who scorned me for not being holy enough in my youth. My holiest of friends embrace me from every part of the cosmos, and my years in monasteries and church socials have shaped me maybe more than the in-crowd mentality of my co-religionists...but who cares?

But, the Jews were in residence today. I saw the generations being channeled today in my longhaired, grey bearded husband. The sun slanted in from the green porch through the barren bougainvillea, and head bowed, glasses pressed against his nose, he studied, he davened, he dove deep into the work before him. Today my Tony revealed himself as the grand son of a rabbi from Warren, Ohio. (Did you know that?)

I could hear his brain mechanisms chanting the pilpul,
"On the one hand" his head seemed to say, but then
"if sixty angels danced on the head of a pin, why now could they not take away one sixtieth of the disease in my lung?"
And so the prayers and reasoning went on and on—quietly conjuring the past seeding the future—on the one hand on the other hand' til he was exhausted and went to lie down with his thoughts.

My husband, the Talmudic scholar, the yeshiva bucher, studying the medical options on his disease, reading the biographies of the patients sliced before him, the outcomes, the measurements. Talking to a friend of a friend in England still weak and struggling through the remnants of the surgery he had two years ago to "cure" his Mesothelioma.

And the chanting, the rocking of all those rabbis in heaven. I could hear them hiding under their dirty Taleisim, praying, snuffling, closing their eyes, stuffing their mouths with herring for inspiration, cleaning their glasses, tipping their heads from side to side to shift the ear wax—-but, ultimately they stayed in the yeshiva of the sky.

They did not come and sit next to my exemplary student, my seeker of the truth, the logician adding inti's and rupiah and trying hard to see how all this adds up to life and hope and possibility. No. They have left him to his own study, his own gathering of information and ultimately to his own leap of faith that will move him where he goes.

For the key to prayer for a Jew is ultimately to integrate and knowledge and then leave the brain behind and ride the soul through the clouds to God—up to where that celestial yeshiva rents space. The job is to ride up kind of like Buzz Lightyear and dance in the clouds and trust the wind and be willing to lose all for the oneness of whatever oneness is.

Sure. Easy, right?

I wonder if Buzz's Super Rocket can give our Tone a lift.

THURSDAY, FEBRUARY 7, 2008
WE'RE MELDING, WE'RE MELDING

There was a fair amount of melding today in our three lives. Curious, as we were all three in different locale.

Me, I wandered the arboretum at Fullerton, the green headed ducks quacking and shaking their heads, just like me. And Sofie, split from chem. and cruised the curves of Mulholland solo and T stayed home deep, deep, and deeper into his own pool of inquiry.

All gasping the same breadth and balancing the exact same radioactivity.

We are traveling this road in synchronistic lock step sensing the hair curves of the road and just like those incredible flocks of boobies we met in the Galapagos last June, who tilt on a diamond cut and weave their wing spreads—soundless and in tune we three dive bomb into our own frenzies of discovery whether we want to or not. Alone. Remarkably in tune.

I remember the years in the Vanities dressing room when we three girls breathed and made that world together. We all three had our moon cycles at exactly the same time, all bleeding and blowing up and making magic as one breathing growl.

And so now, despite adolescent angst, and midlife restlessness and exhaustion from too much accomplishment on his back, we three are one. Weaving and darting, sailing the updrafts and roller coaster stomach drops without saying a word.

Such is love. Such is love. Clarity is approaching but it is not without cost.

SATURDAY, FEBRUARY 9, 2008
TO SLEEP PERCHANCE TO DREAM

What do you do when you get what you want,
but you want what you get to be better,
but you'll take what you get
for the sake of the bet and forsake
what you thought could unfetter
the long, long days of hard, hard work
ah to rest, to sleep, to sleep perchance to dreammmmmmmmm

Last night pursued by the dark skinned fellows again all through the streets of New York.
Nothing unusual, just exhausting and a recurrent dream for him for years now. Almost caught in the streets of New York.

And, T had been dreaming of singing. Yes, all last week, he would smile and turn in our bed and a long low wail of rock and roll and guitar riff would dribble from his mouth, eyes closed, eyebrows lifted in delight. I thought it was pain or horror, no offense to his dream state composition intended, but he would wake, having slept well AND having garnered rave reviews from the gathering in his head. All those angels gathering to welcome him home. Perhaps preparing his own little rock spot of fame in heaven's Chelsea loft BUT not right now, fellas.

Yes has come from the heavens like Groucho's duck quacking it's clatter and saying" not yet, suckah!!"

There's a whole lot of yes-sing going on.
"Yes," says Dr. Gupta, beautiful Indian eyes leveled at ours, yesterday in the surgeon's retreat.

"Yes", the make up of the cells on the biopsy slides are 90% Epithelioid, That's the good kind,
and YES you do not have cancer in the LEFT lung—that was inflammation
and YES, you DO have more intense cancer on the right lung
but YES that cancer is most likely in the pleura and not the lung
and YES, they can and will peel away the pleural tumor
and YES, it will be an 8-12 hour surgery
but YES there is only a 1% risk of mortality since there is no invasion of major organs,
and YES, they no longer do the other originally proposed surgery which would have taken the lung and had left the friend of a friend in England T spoke to barely breathing two years since,
but YES it was too barbaric a surgery and the survival rates are now found to be the same between that surgery and this
and YES, the Atrial fib may be a problem, but
YES, they can handle that with drips in the ICU and
YES, that may mean that the four—count them, four tubes
sprouting from his chest may have to be in place a few days longer but
YES, T will probably be home within 5-7 days and YES, he will rest for about a month
(here's where the visiting and the food train comes in, guys)
and YES there will be radiation and
YES maybe even chemo after that but

YES it's not as bad as it once was and survival median rates are around 2-3 years or more—that gets us through Sofie's graduation
YES—we even have a happy and RICH survivor of the surgery right here in the next little cubicle.

And in walks Mr. D Von H who is not slouching or slurring or moaning. He looks fairly sharp in his loafers and yellow button down shirt and he tells us his story of his terminal diagnosis, inoperable, not a chance—just like T, and how his wife found Cameron on the internet like we did and how he had the operation in June and he looked perfectly fine and he just dropped off a major check for the Pacific Heart and Lung Institute because not only is he alive and looking spiffy he just got a settlement check from his lawyers of TEN MILLION dollars. Hmmmmm. Now isn't that interesting??

Now, T hates yellow button down shirts and the details about the ten million may not grace our story but it's a nice touch to his, don't you think?

So, swoop, swallow, gulp, change gears and stay the course because it's not over yet and then there is more living to do and that can be as tough as sailing over to the great beyond, perhaps.

But, he's made the leap of faith and in about three weeks, maybe early March after our next First Sunday gathering and he's banked enough blood out so his own blood can be transfused back in, the next phase commences—at UCLA. So stay tuned.

There will be depositions and cardiologists before that, and God knows what else, but it certainly isn't dull.
xxoo

TUESDAY, FEBRUARY 12, 2008
SILENCE

…is golden sometimes.

Adjusting to the news of Friday has left us silent. A lot of thinking about survival and its costs, its benefits, its adjustments and its demands.

Besides a busy agenda of work and avoidance, silence has changed the landscape as there is a big long whistling corridor called the future that is hard to people, to focus or grasp.

Tony is dreaming again, this time of piles of multiplying powders like the starry night talc heaved into his right lung to let it breathe during the biopsy like the cancer that keeps piling up in the pleura.

And we got the date today, 28 February for the surgery at UCLA.
Many tests and measurements, documents and assurances between now and then.

Legal, medical and spiritual hurdles. About ten days in the hospital they say to wait 'til the lung no longer leaks and can hold the air that bellows it and then home to rest and heal some more and then we shall see how the body withstands and the spirit fulfils the task.

It is no small thing to contemplate any future but one uncertain and mixed with reality has all sorts of colors. No need for Pollyanna and her "glad game." We can find much to be happy about, but it's those lurking rainbow prisms that shed surprising light and color that hold the most interesting of gifts, Garish in their promise, elusive prisms. Translucent perhaps or channeling light into laser. Digging in, raw.

Just what part of the reality sandwich shall we land in is not quite clear we have to listen to the silence along with the bruiting ballyhoo and continue our marigold journey.

I like to think of the hands of the surgeon. In the photos you can see his hands coaxing tumor off lung, cajoling it to peel itself back and away from healthy meat. I like the way his hand looks in that picture, holding the heart of the man he promised to save. It's strong like the sculptor, feeling the tissue for a clue to its release like Michaelangelo did with angels from their slab.

Remember walking thru that gallery in Florence and seeing the way life grew from rock?

I remember that. Let's remember that.

THURSDAY, FEBRUARY 14, 2008
DAY OF THE HEART

… and true to its title, T spent the day with the Head of Cardiology at UCLA.

A lovely fellow who pronounced him fit and hearty for the journey ahead—except for a slight retake of a test or two—but fine just fine to float on.

It's like navigating a very long frigate into healthy harbor, this surgery preparation. Dropping off fuel for the return ride—the transfusions. And getting the tug to pull just right—the heart engine. And making sure the bilge pump is ready to rid the innards of the stuff not needed for ballast. And all those nautical references.

And then, we three ate garlic chicken and calamari at Versailles tonight and onions and bananas and chatted. Just the simple stuff. A conversation about school and what makes a heart healthy on Valentines day—like what makes the heart happy and worthy—what makes a life well lived.

And Sof says;
"Love. Loving. That's what I want to accomplish in this life. Loving and being loved and so far so good."

And us, mama and papa, grin the botox grin at and thru each other— that is, our faces moving no discernible muscle. Ah! To hear the words and feel the feeling! Receiving the love, receiving the heart healthy gift of a kid who knows the value of giving and receiving same, especially this year. Especially all of us together and you too, our blogster family.

Happy Valentine's Day. May we all learn the joy and fear of giving and receiving love, and let that whack us thru the energy fields for that's what'll sustain all dimensions.

"To infinity and beyond"...thank you once again, dear Buzz.

MONDAY, FEBRUARY 18, 2008
NO NEWS

...is good news...isn't it?

Frankly, we haven't a clue. It seems odd that after such drama of the last six weeks that things have settled into a dull, damp rhythm of hospital tests and too much detail debris and calming others fears and back to the basics. But we are moving thru the days with no idea whether terror and end of planet planning is in order or just adjusting to the next thing, which will lead to the next thing, which will lead to the next.

T is in good spirits, a little tired, a little pissed to have to be doing all this shit, when he'd much rather just snooze, but he is dutifully leaving bits of himself in various labs and x ray machines around the west side. I am wrangling with insurance people and setting up agreements that may be moot., looking for more teaching hours to bank against the coming cuts at Cal State—my savior in the health insurance world the last months and now not sure how long they can sustain my job—(YIKES). Ideas welcome!

Sofie is pulling up her grades and doing the good stuff of being a junior in high school, and we enjoyed a major frenzy of cousins and food this weekend again.

And life is good and bad and all the things it is for all of us.

There are a few glitches in some tests, and there will be a few adjustments here and there I suppose, but the adrenalin of making it to the next 30 seconds seems to have eased for today.

Tony is dreaming his dreams again. I believe there was pink and purple pee-ing in the snow the other night, while holding umbrellas at a jaunty angle for two Japanese dancers dressed in the same pink and purple colors—candy stripers, oooh. And last night leaning against a juke box in his dreams singing
"I'd like to go to heaven, just not right now," with the appropriate twang… and isn't that just exactly where we all are?

Stay tuned for more drama, but today we are on easy listening and trying to get some rest.

xxoo

WEDNESDAY, FEBRUARY 20, 2008
YOU GOTTA KNOW WHEN TO HOLD 'EM

While lying on a massage table last night, breathing deep to help the thumbs of the able Anthony to release my neck and skull from the power grip of: "Fine, fine, everything is just fine, thank you," I got to thinking about what is worth holding on to, what is worth letting go of, and the wisdom to know the difference.

There's love, always good to hang on to. If you can figure out what it is and who is really delivering the goods. And there's resentment—good to get rid of, but sometimes great to hang on to. when one needs a wound or two to lick, and then there's what you learned in kindergarten sometimes worth it and sometimes a pile of crap—

But then if you're supposed to let go of things, how come the body holds on for dear life, or clutch of death spasm to the point of illness or reformation? And if we are supposed to trust the universe, then how come the universe continues to confound us with lessons that give only the most enlightened the clues with which to proceed?

This takes me back to that thought about the punishing god a few weeks back…the one that says "kneel and tremble" rather than "ah babe it's all gonna be okay."

I recently have been lucky enough to spend time in NYC again, my spiritual home, in my spiritual sprouting place, that rusty theater on 52nd street, and I have had the distinct pleasure of seeing faces come up those stairs that I have not seen for over thirty years.

As each face climbed the stairs and came into view I had to push aside the years and find the spark holding them to their essential selves, the selves that I know and that know me and there they are…still there, still holding onto the life spark given to them and still giving that life spark to me. That's a good holding, one that multiplies.

And then there's the grab of my old aunt at my Dad's funeral, who wouldn't let me see my father's body for the last time, and chose instead to envelop me with her pain rather than let me have my own.. Now that was bad holding.

I think it's what Jean Paul Sartre said: "now and then I feel the caress of time as it goes by."

And it's what I feel in my neck clawing into my nerves so very close, holding on for dear life in every muscle cell and atom to what I want to be true to the picture I visualize everyday to the happy family and good times we are stockpiling.

Head trust is fine, therapy helps, so does life and intellect. But wild, primal trust, that sometimes comes with a lover… that trust—to release completely into what is…that is a path to be sought and then balance between taut attention and flaccid surrender.

We love and hope and laugh and ignore and then, just like King Kong, God picks us up by our teeny tiny feet, wiggles us around and says, just like my sad and crazy mama once did "go ahead, kid, live. I dare you."

It ain't so bad but it gives you a run for your money.

MONDAY, FEBRUARY 25, 2008
PROFUNDIS ABSENTIA

So, I figure I better check in with everyone, as we close in on the date. Yep, despite living and feeling better than he has in a few years, making us really feel the total absurdity of this fact, this Thursday, the 28th of Feb— is the date for Tony's surgery.

Tony has had a great time the last two months! So much celebrating, two Lakers games, a night at Disney Hall, crowds at MOCA, countless bottles of scotch, homemade spaghetti, Oscars and pizza and ice cream ice cream ice cream—gourmet, hand delivered, cheap and fabulous galore. SOOOO many thank yous to all providers. It has been a jolly, chubbifying time— and, thanks to the careful placement of that talc in his lungs during the biopsy, an easy breathing time as well. And let's not forget that the rhythm gods have restored his heart to sinus rhythm for some reason or other after seven years.

So, despite all evidence to the contrary, it is true that T still has a life-threatening cancer and the magic surgeon is going to go in and dig it out by hand.

Here's a run down again for those who haven't been following the blog. He goes in Thursday, they slice, select a lymph node or two to sample, they sew, he wakes, they rearrange the 4-6 tubes coming out of him at a tasteful angle, drug him heavily, he goes back to sleep. This goes on for a few yucky days, I am told. Then, miraculously, he begins to feel human again, and they move him from one unit to another and he begins the process of letting his wounds heal and his lung get used to not leaking air. This can take anywhere from 5-10 days depending on how windy he might or might not be.

Then he comes home, sleeps a lot, rests, chats with friends, watches bad movies, takes more drugs and generally chants to the healing gods to make him feel better—once that is over—about a month—then, he goes into radiation which feels like internal sunburns we've been told. Then…depending on the state of the tasty lymph nodes, he gears up for

4 months of chemo. Once that is ALLLLLLLLL OVERRRRRRRRR and he is still standing (hopefully) then he goes on interferon every day for the rest of his life. Sound like fun? You bet.

So, we are in for it, and will proceed as we have proceeded thus far, one inch at a time.

We have plenty of food, thank you.
Once Tony comes home, stay tuned for visiting ops, and so it goes.

Sofie had her 17th birthday yesterday…
The guest bathroom is almost finished.
I will be at UCLA during the next week with T.
Email is fine. I will not be answering the phone.
But will update the blog every day that there is something to say.

Pray for steady hands and great drugs.
xxoo

WEDNESDAY, FEBRUARY 27, 2008
PRE OPENING JITTERS

…forgive the pun but…
We show up at 5 AM tomorrow at UCLA and surgery to commence at 7:30.

We are so very, very grateful for the SCORES of messages of good will and good cheer and prayer circles and all the great and noble lofts of love that are floating our way, most especially T's way as we move out of the celebratory mode to the real deal of survival.

I would be lying if I said there are no jitters, but I also need to tell everyone that the heaps of ice cream and scotch and love and joy and gourmet meals et al have changed T for the good. Truly for the good.

We all need the boost now and then of realizing our value in relation to the many with whom we live and love, and T has received such a strong and steady outpouring of yes and yes and yes that it has changed and refueled him for the long and arduous task ahead.

Tomorrow we start the long haul and we will continue the one-inch at a time policy, which has served us well—as the wise cousin Betsy said at the beginning of the road, "this is a marathon" and we are just about to approach the first hill.

So thank you for your love, support, friendship and goodness, you are known and acknowledged and you have made our life the last two months a wonder of strange hope in the midst of madness.

T's afternoon nap of fatigue will give way to longer rests I imagine, but we have no idea what is next except for that we move into it, well cushioned with as much ammo as possible.

So, stay tuned to the blog, I will update as often as I can.
I won't answer the phone, but will return email as best I can.

much love

THURSDAY, FEBRUARY 28, 2008
THE DAY, THE MOMENT, THE UPDATE LIVE

I think the best bet is to do updates as I have them today:

It was dark at 4:30 AM when we tooled down Melrose and debated the possibility of hitting PCH and just keep driving. But T said, "nope, let's give it a shot"—and good he said that because once he arrived here at UCLA he got plenty—Of shots-Of needles, that is. IV's everywhere but a competent crew. A lotta eager young beavers a la Grey's Anatomy…

There was a problem with the ProTyme level, that is the level of coagulation in his blood because he hadn't been told to stop the Coumadin (anticoagulant) early enough—so…they had to give him a drip of the jello stuff to make it all shake and shimmy correctly in his veins.

The pain team is quite nice and competent—and they have nice hats—green patterns here and there. There's the uptight, small eye-glassed chief watching his underlings like a hawk, the passive Asian pain second (that's what they call him) who watches everything and nods wisely, then the really smart 'Sandra Oh with the edge' assistant who did most of the sticking. Shultz's Anatomy: anticipating a long and healthy run.

They are probably opening him up just about now and peeling, peeling the lining away.
Okay. I'm going to lunch and will check in with you when I have more news.

Thanks for all the sweet messages. We are fine. We are begun.

xxoo

THURSDAY, FEBRUARY 28, 2008
UPDATE MIDDAY

Tall Doctor Cameron, with his gentle manner and diamond stud in his left ear, surprisingly came out to see me on the patio here at UCLA about half hour ago.

The operation itself was going well, the tumor was peeling back from the lung nicely, but there is a problem in that Tony's blood pressure is very low, so low that it is not responding to Epenepherine or the other drugs, and so low that the doctor did not want to continue the operation. So, they have closed Tony back up, are keeping him sedated and intubated in the operating room, and are trying to figure out what the problem is. It may be an allergic reaction to the drugs in combination. They have no idea.

We are in a holding pattern. They are trying to figure out the cause of the problem before they proceed so they can fix it. It may mean that they will need to wait 'til the drugs wear off to figure out what to do, and then go back in to finish the cancer operation when they know.

Omigod.
Love.
Stay tuned.

THURSDAY, FEBRUARY 28, 2008
PHEW!

Okay— so...it looks like the Pain Team inserted the epidural catheter in the wrong place...ooops... and that seems to have caused the blood pressure to plummet—

Yeah duh.... okay, okay.

It happens VERY rarely,

all of that,

no comment.

But, T has not awakened and they are going in to complete the operation at this moment—pray for better luck this time around. It is now quarter to 5 and Sofie is coming by for dinner and I will hang here 'til T is out of surgery about 10 tonight. And then hopefully he will awaken refreshed and renewed...

Stay tuned.
Much love.

THURSDAY, FEBRUARY 28, 2008
ALLS WELL THAT ENDS WELL, THIS EVE AT LEAST

So the tall and stately Dr. Cameron, soft handed and softer-spoken, came forth from the operating room about ten minutes ago, and the remainder of the surgery went well. No further problems. He is breathing on his own and they will keep him in the recovery room overnight to keep an eye on him, because he had trouble earlier.

I will get a chance to see him in a bit, and then head home to sleep. Now, to rest and heal and wait for the return of the lymph nodes in about a week. The witness team here all day staggering out with me in a few minutes or so. No visitors here yet.

A quiet day or two until we know how he will heal, and then we will proceed to the next inch.

Sleep well.

We've made it this far, with a little bit of help from our friends....on this side and the other.
love

xxoo

FRIDAY, FEBRUARY 29, 2008
THE MERRY PRANKSTER AND HIS WIFE

Phew…
Okay all,
Here we go,

Spent the night waiting for T to come up from recovery. He arrived at the ICU around 3 AM with fairly interesting hallucinations and a fairly interesting tangle of transformer tubes—dangling at all angles.

He kept telling me to "stop the prank now," and to "get him his guitar" and that I "was a very good actor, but I needed to stop the prank because I was causing him serious pain"—

Indeed, there was an understatement. The pain was and is major but we got one of the magic pumps and that helped last night and now— It seems his fantasy was that I had rented this hospital set, hired all these people to dress up as doctors as a birthday prank to surprise him. That there really was no surgery but something had gone terribly wrong because he was hurting terribly and if I just called off the prank everything would be just fine...Hmmmmm.

Once I disabused him of that idea, things got sorted out, and I headed home around 8 AM to sleep for a few hours. Back here around 2 and he was moved from ICU into a teeny tiny double room—which I got changed into a larger fab room and like that.

Josh—Tony's great friend and great doctor—dropped in to make sure all was okay. The surgeons are on it—wonderful nurse Julie and care partner Berenice. Everyone has been good.

Word from the surgeon is that there was no gross evidence of tumor on the lung itself. We await pathology on lymph nodes, but there was no need for removing any of the lung itself... Excellent news there.

Pain is tough, but he is resting now and it seems he is doing just fine. He'll be here at least 'til Tuesday and probably no guests 'til Sunday so check in with me before you drop in—okay?

So many thanks to the so many of you who are calling and writing and sending love. We are on the road and as always, I will keep you updated.

SATURDAY, MARCH 1, 2008
MIGHTY PAIN AND MEAT THERMOMETERS

Rougher today. Got here at hospital by 10:30. They are balancing meds and Atrial fib sneaking in now and then and blood pressure stuff.

The pain is mighty and that's the real tale, the Pain Team have their hands full, but they have managed to do fairly well—the threesome trolling the hall with secret smiles wielding the magic that everyone craves.

T continues his imitation of a loopy Marlon Brando in the Godfather. This from the windy lung not yet adhered to the chest wall, which is where it is heading to seal. Hard to rest and get comfortable and not hard to imagine why.

I caught a tasty look at the incision and the three chest tubes neatly slid into his flesh like little meat thermometers measuring the heat of the flesh. Ouch, ouch, ouch.

Ate only two things—you can guess what—raspberry sorbet and raspberry sorbet—it's a waiting game…

Not yet ready for human presentation
Stay tuned.
Love
s

SUNDAY MORNING 10:30 AM

Well—day started a little better with T managing to sit up in a chair for about ten minutes and a pretty good breakfast, but he is in such pain and still quite loopy.. Pouring sweat, all of that. Latest visitor—from the other realms—is tall large black man in white robes who seems to be seated nearby, nodding every now and then. He says others keep poking their heads in to say hello.

All the docs have been thru and they will continue to keep an eye on everything, keep the fluids draining, the heart beating a little less wildly, and the blood pressure up—see, if he would have had higher blood pressure to start then it would be good it dropped so much…

They weighed him this morning and I think they said he is carrying up to ten pounds of extra liquid.

A hospital night of sleep complete with chest x rays at 4 AM. Night nurses giggling with x-ray techs. Too much explanation at every medication or what ever was needed. That being said, everyone is trying their best to balance all the elements and hopefully he will be better inch by inch…

I stayed with him last night. Cousin KB with Sof at home. Will get a little break this afternoon but he is still not ready for visitors.
Next week maybe.
Much love and thanks for all your messages and prayers.
s

MONDAY MARCH 3, 2008
ROUGH WATERS, STEADY SAILING

Today was a real tough one. The pain seems to be managed but the desperate details are making themselves known.

Had to come home last night to spend time with Sof and T was confused and a sad isolate when I got back there this morning. He is disoriented with anyone else still.

Terrible time finding veins for IVs. Efforts totaling over an hour and a half—and too many technicians. Finally the masterful Evelyn (do we think the angels were at work there) and Obed managed to get the new lines in and the blood out.

Yesterday, they decided that there were too many drugs and sedatives so they decided that the panic meds had to go and that of course resulted in—guess what—yes, of course panic.

After much clear but measured insistence to all involved (in case you don't know me, I am understating here) including patient relations and various others we got the Klonapin back and that helped to soothe the rough waters, hopefully.

They had to do a blood transfusion—hence the new IV lines, and that is now done and we shall see if that helps. Otherwise the rest of the stuff seems to be balancing a bit but it is like riding a rough sea in a steady ship,

The captain and mates are doing what they can to keep the passengers safe and secure despite mighty waves and resulting nausea. Something like that.

I hope he can rest and sleep thru the night as I think I can only be at one place at one time. Perhaps I should suggest that my daughter and/or my husband should hallucinate me allowing me to double and show up wherever seems best.

Okay, tomorrow I have a few appointments and will be in and out of UCLA and that will correspond with a better day for T, I sure hope.

I have Thursday coverage for T when I go to Fullerton to teach and not sure when he will be home but probably not 'til end of week if then...

He still needs to sit up in a chair a bit more, keep the lungs clearing, walk the long halls, eat a full meal, breathe without oxygen, keep his blood pressure up on his own, have a better blood count, make friends with the tall black man in the white robes.

He watches the clock—minute by minute, informing me how long it has been since he has slept and how many minutes until the next meal, which he isn't eating. And wondering who is singing to him in the silence. I'd like to know that myself.

We are making progress.
I am tempting him with ice cream.
He is a mighty warrior and doing what he can.
The docs are in there too as well as nurses and care partners.
It's a good effort and we shall see how it continues

And then...if this was the whole thing... I haven't even contemplated what comes next

Nope—not tonight.
Inch by inch.
We are indeed getting by with a great deal of help from our friends. Blessings all round.
s

TUESDAY, MARCH 4, 2008
EXTREME MAKEOVER SHULTZ MERSON EDITION

It was a day of many masks, happy sad and sanguine. Lots of good angel friends. There in an instant to cover T during two appointments today and last night too when I had to go home.

He was distraught and very anxious last night, and seems to be having that problem sundowners…know that one—happens in the eve to folk. I know it only too well from years with my mom. The anxiety more pronounced in evening and after a day of wonderfully creative hallucinations for T. It has been pretty exhausting for the boy.

Jane reports that there was a Jerusalem Summit in the room this morning before I got here and she was covering…and it was a good thing too because when I did arrive after my morning appointment, T says: "Isn't that something?"
"Yes, indeed….", waiting for the punch-line, I.
"I'm the president," he says.
"Really."
"We have to move to the White House, Susie."
"Okay," I say. "As long as I don't have to host any teas."

And various other stripes appearing throughout the day, his brain constantly at work trying to figure himself out thru the fog of Delaudid and other meds, and breathing treatments and all of that—preventing him from resting much. He is enjoying the fact that Dr. Cameron came in and said that he is healing nicely and hopefully he will have a tube out on Thursday and another soon after.
Good news indeed.

Mickey covered in the afternoon when I hurried to another appointment, passing the waiting families in the waiting area downstairs, stern sentinels, camped out wondering how they got there, making the chairs all their own for today only to relinquish them to the next group of waiting families the next day and the next.

Such are hospitals and when they work well, as does this one, they are also peopled by smart faces, right there, attentive and strong. They hear us and see us and it has made a great difference in this journey. The nursing staff has been remarkable. The heart girls, as Tony calls the thoracic, cardiac doctors who make morning rounds (only one lone male intern—T always partial to smart pretty girls), the pain team, the Cameron magic makers, the residents and care partners. There are a lot of good hearts around here with open ears, good hearts.

And returning here to the hospital, after getting a call from my agent telling me I GOT one of the jobs I have been auditioning for in order to assure us health insurance from now 'til then since T is no longer insurable by new carriers and I am not vested at Cal State and so the cobra there will leave us high and dry if I lose that job with state cuts.

And me WEEPING in the car, when my agent told me the news after leaving yet another audition—the third in three days—the third after nothing for over a year! These appointments being set up by a wonderful old friend who has made calls on my behalf to other casting folk to get me the appointments after all this time—the agents, the casting people I have worked with diffidently and defensively for twenty something years. all heaping rewards on my plate. Coming thru like champs. I started to WEEP like those people on Extreme Makeover Home Edition because my husband DOES have cancer, (blubber, blubber)and he IS in the hospital totally wrecked, (blubber) and we ARE looking at some rocky days ahead (WAIL WEEP)and I am so DEEPLY GRATEFUL to everyone who is helping us so much.

I just lost it on the phone in my husband's car like those people on the TV program that I am always so embarrassed watching while Michael my agent—just like that guy on Queen for A Day used to do—told me he got me a good rate, and a great dressing room and I was on the road toward insurance. Well...you can imagine, and then I was back at the hospital.

Tony has been shifting and restless all night and just now tried to make a beeline to the bathroom and got himself tangled in all the wires...and, let's see there were four or five folk in here trying to fix that...

Well—that's enough for now. We are continuing to make it with a lotta help from all of our friends. Man oh man. Love and thanks and good night.

THURSDAY, MARCH 6, 2008
ROUGH RIDING AT RONALD REAGAN

Did you know that UCLA Med Center is the Ronald Reagan Medical Center?

What is the difference between getting an airport named for you or a hospital? This is something to be pondered at a later date.

It is now Thursday and the last 48 hours have been immensely challenging.

The good news is that the surgeon removed two of the four chest tubes this morning. The heart is still in A fib and that remains challenging, but blood pressure seems to be okay and his physical strength is returning. Walked the halls twice today and sat in his chair most of the afternoon.

The mood still is enormously troubling, stemming from the Klonapin withdrawal, the Dilaudid, the stress etc. He has not slept for several nights. I worked today and understand that he didn't speak all day, which frankly is not so bad after several days of restless and delusional talk. Who was it said that the drugs were great?
Hmmm.

They are now working on getting his mood stabilized. He is calm, too calm, saying little, watching everything, whispering to me in private only. More than the regular delusional stuff from Dilaudid. We are into another realm at the moment of quiet and watchful paranoia. And now complete and utter exhaustion which may work to his advantage finally and allow him to sleep.

We still have sitters to stay with him when I can not be there and a few close pals cover him as well, quietly remaining as anchors during this odd and fluid time.

Probably at least another 4-5 days here but I will try to get him strong enough to get him outside on the plazato get a little sun and feel a little wind on his skin over the weekend.

He has always been a guy who needs sunshine.

xxoo

TURNED A CORNER

Am too tired to write but we have turned a corner today and I think things will steadily improve. Stay tuned.
xxoo
s

FRIDAY, MARCH 7, 2008
I HARDLY KNOW…

…how to begin to tell you what the last two and half days have been like.

Suffice to say there has been high drama, low comedy and major confrontation with bureaucratic authority. Unfortunately, or fortunately—one must be a warrior advocate for a loved one while in a hospital.

This does not make one the winner of Ms. Congeniality. It does make one suspect to the bureaucracy. It does help enormously to have a loud mouth, New York shoulders, and a sincere thank you, and smile. It does help to yelp and wail at authorities and rattle as many buckets and bells as you can without getting arrested. It does help to love the person you are going to bat for fiercely. It does help to store up brownie points with those in the power structure who can help resolve a matter...but also to know that it makes little difference in major entrenched institutions.

There are structures in place in UCLA to deal with problems, but unfortunately the wheels are slow and full of shit and false smiles and basically—in our case, the hospital came up a day late and a dollar short on T's latest healing crisis.

Thanks instead to the noble efforts of floor nurses who helped him thru the nights, kind care partner-ism who mopped his brow and bathed him sweetly, a Zen like surgical team, who appreciated the silence he chose for awhile, Evelyn and Mickey Shultz up in heaven for whatever they were doing and a good dose of fuck you—touch him again and I'll kill you from his gentle and well mannered spouse.

My god, where goes gentility when one fights to protect someone you love from an unseen foe and frankly I began to feel as paranoid as my sweet nut case husband after a while.

But ...NOW...today T slept for the first time in five days. He is walking, talking, making more sense, beginning to rest and make progress and my job is to keep him safe until I can get him home.

Man oh man.

With all best intentions things happen. Risk is everywhere. They're making lists, checking them twice. Sound familiar???

How's that for persistent mystery.
xxoo
s

SATURDAY, MARCH 8, 2008
RIP VAN WINKLE AWAKES

Yes. He is back.

Wondering where he has been the last 9 days, finally emerging from the fog of ill administered drugs. Everything from the misplaced epidural during surgery to the removal of a longtime med causing a severe drug withdrawal reaction that sent him spinning into outer space for almost 48 hours with NO RESPONSE from the UCLA Psych team, or T's less than gracious psychiatrist. But even with wonderful response from insider doctors and friends of friends doctors and my screaming and threatening and raging at the jerks and the nurses requesting help—still NOTHING to help T for 48 long hours…long, long hours of looking at the clock and listing the items in the room and…no matter or matter for lawsuits only. Now, to revel in his return.

His opinions returning, requests, and restlessness for return of full health. All possible, all good. all reasonable and then they tried to put him back on delusional meds yesterday when he was feeling fine! Now who's cuckoo and what nest are we talking about?

No. Now just Tylenol for pain, and it's working fine, thank you.

And I am just left fuming but…had a good massage today and am moving on. Yeah right.

Okay. The news. Tony is getting through the crisis. He has two tubes left that are still leaking air, so he is not quite ready to come home. They are suggesting Tuesday-ish. We are beginning low level visits this week at the hospital. Check in to let me know if you'd like to stop by. No word on pathology yet but frankly, that's fine. No more input needed for now. The wheels are still spinning from this latest speed away from disaster.

Attention must be paid, friends.

SUNDAY, MARCH 9, 2008
MAGNIFICENCE, A TRIBUTE

As we all know, or we learn as we grow, we absolutely cannot move through a full life without the interaction and weaving of lives. And being a bossy woman, I admire many others of the same ilk... say, Hillary Clinton—(it's why she'll be a great bossy president that we need, but that's another thing)

But because I admire bossy women I seek out, revere and learn enormous amounts from the legions of enormously valuable and well tested women (and men too) who have gathered round us and linked fingers and toes and humor and fierceness and said:
"Fuck you! We're here and we're going nowhere.

We have seen children born with neurological challenges, and husbands transferring body fluids from cell to cell and wars fought illegally and protested. We have born children near and far, dealt with addictions, lost parents and lovers and siblings and friends, lived through divorce, met long lost fathers and mothers after years of no contact, we have done the right thing and the only thing and true thing—and we have taken the messy consequences and we are standing strong and firm and defiant... and it's no big deal. "It's what we do."

These fierce women (and men) of our community.

I am deeply moved by that. By this weaving of fabric that each of us contributes to with humor and grace and toughness and clear eyes and soup and sympathy and tough talk and house cleaning and new dishes and fabulous flowers and all the things that are necessary
now—at this time—at all times.

We are a community that knows what's necessary and Tony and I and Sof count ourselves as one with this community, and we are honored to receive and to give all those things.

This morning a few of these honored magnificent ones gathered to shout politics and diets and opinions at each other, while my fabulously growing daughter sat and got what it is to be a magnificent woman...and that was really something. I am grateful but more than that—I am charged—we are charged at this time of our lives with the responsibility of being true and full and we have taken this on together and this mantle is no small thing.

We need to feel this feeling of being one and heaving ourselves together and apart up and through. We are all honored to simply be doing what needs to be done and that is extraordinary.

I never believed it possible. It is what our marriage has given me.

Okay

I arrived at the hospital to see Tony still here ministered to by yet another beautiful friend and we are on the road. Yes, indeed. It gets simpler every day.

Okay then. Count on me. We are still walking the marathon. Pathology report back but we won't know what it says 'til tomorrow. I had almost forgotten that there was more to this than just postoperative resurrection.

Stay tuned
love
s

MONDAY, MARCH 10, 2008
AhHHHHHHhhhHHHHH....!

Lymph nodes clear

recovery
recovery
recovery

radiation
radiation

interferon
interferon and on on on on and

life straight ahead.

Omigod
I have to get back to pilates class.

xxoo
s

TUESDAY MARCH 11, 2008
THE SLANT OF THE LATE AFTERNOON SUN

…just dappled. Truly, like in those poems.

The slanted afternoon light, dappled by the leaves fell so softly thru our bedroom windows. The jasmine scent wafted in to cushion the scene and T took a deep sigh and got into our bed around 5 this afternoon, and has been sleeping sleeping sleeping thru the sunset and brisket left by excellent elves for dinner.

So we are home and gathered, our threesome. Resting, resting, resting. Grateful.
Sh-hh-h-h-h-h

Sofie is readying herself for ten days in Rome with her girlfriend (poor child) and we will settle back into our rhythm here.

T cannot speak yet and is still not ready for visits and I am buried in paperwork and catching up but I do need some help with sitters in the next weeks now and then, so if you're free and want to volunteer to just be here. no chatting, just being here just let me know by email and I will see if I can slip you into a slot.

Please do make contact before just dropping in.

So many thanks for all your help.
s

SATURDAY MARCH 15, 2008
THE GREAT SADNESS OF THE IDES OF MARCH

Dearest friends,
this you will not believe
there is such sadness and surprise
today

T came home from the hospital
on Tuesday evening,
he was doing well though in a great deal of pain.
He was nauseous,
so nauseous and in such pain
but strong, fortified
ready to live,

but then there was shortness of breath
and the nausea didn't subside
and there was no sleep
no rest to be had
around every corner there was pain and
illness and it was a difficult few days

and we went to the doctors and he made it thru that
and the nausea would not leave him
and he needed so to rest
and he could find no rest and then finally

I got him Compazine and there were the other things he needed
and finally last night after many tries

I settled him in our bed, the pillows stacked, and puffed to support him
so he could breathe and perhaps allay the nausea
and he closed his eyes,
and good, I thought
I thought oh good, relief,
and I lay with him for a little but he
kept startling,
so I closed the door slightly and told him
I was going to rest and I went into the other room and lay down and

I checked on him at midnight and then at 2 and at 4 and at 4 he
was lying on his side, curled up, oxygen on, his eyes closed and
I thought oh good, to rest, to sleep at last and
then I checked on him at 6 and at 8 and he was still sleeping and

at 9:15 again and then the sunlight was streaming in the window and
he was grey, green and cold so cold to the touch
and I closed the door and thought, "I cannot see him breathing"
and he was not breathing
and I called for him and I held him
and I shook him and he was gone and

I called 911
and he was gone and they told me to try CPR but
he was gone and I called to him and he was gone
and his face was peaceful and his eyes were closed and
our darling Tony
our friend
our love our stellar man of integrity
and truth
our Tony Shultz was gone.

Bushwahacked, I think,
surprised to go in his sleep.

Not expecting it but peaceful on his face.
They say righteous men die in their sleep
and so our T.

9:15 AM, the ides of March 2008.
he is gone
and we are here
and we are weeping and feeling the wind sweep the skies

the hearse took him away at exactly 11 AM. and the bells,
yes actually really,
the bells rang out as he went down the street
wrapped in our quilt that I made of silk scarves from the
Van Gogh exhibit so long ago and his first Hawaiian shirts

our darling friends
our beloved community
our Tony is gone.

Sof is in Italy and we must bring her home
with her cousin by Wednesday and
we will probably gather to celebrate Tony and his life
on Friday of this next week.

And we will sing and weep and
celebrate our darling man
as the winds sweep the sky and
the sun showers speak to me to tell me that he is safe
though sad to be far away.
So very sad that he is far away

My love to you all.
My heart is yours.
More news will follow.

Sh-h-h-h-h
breathe for us

for yourselves
news will be here

amen

SUNDAY MARCH, 2008
THIS THURSDAY AT 12 NOON

Dear friends

we will gather at the Mt. Sinai Mortuary
on Forest lawn Drive just before you hit the 134 and the back end of Griffith Park.

12 noon Thursday
Tony will be there and you can see him if you choose to. I feel it is important for me to see the body and feel him gone feel the closure of his departure but if you feel otherwise, please do not feel you need to come forward. During this time there will be music from his nephew, Max Williams, on Tony's guitar

My love to you all. I look forward to meeting those friends of Tony that I have yet to meet. Please do spread the word to friends and colleagues. Tony would love it if all the seats were filled!

Much love and many, many thanks
susan

TUESDAY MARCH 18, 2008
SPINNING SPINNING AND NEW DETAILS

At 6 AM today I found myself on the set of a bizarre and wonderful vampire television series whispering sweet nasties into the face of a grown and now blonde Anna Paquin.

Yes, my husband not yet settled in heaven, my daughter not yet returned from Rome, the legions of lovers marching toward us as we head toward our conflagration of love and sadness celebrating the beauty of my partner and our friend.
Don't ask—

It was Friday. He was so uncomfortable. Still barely speaking, drinking little, eating nothing, sucking oxygen:
"Tony, Monday I do that vampire thing. Shall I do the vampire thing?"
His eyes roll, disgusted. "Of course. Yes. Do the vampire thing."

And our Sof calls from the airport as she steps on a plane for Rome, her great adventure and I translate for her Dad "have a spectacular time sweetheart. Enjoy your wonderful adventure. I love you. You are a terrific girl and I am so very proud of you."
"I love you daddy."
"I love you sweetheart."

The simplicity of endings, the banality of bliss.

All these things spinning, spinning and the wind whipping us to the west a long drive with Keith Jarrett, wailing in the wind in Tony's Audi today, blessedly alone, windy and trying to hard to fit the wind— friends in the twilight eating chopped liver and jambalaya, 58 messages on my email.

Planning the funeral yesterday, the funeral director telling us we can really get a better deal on real estate if we bury T in Simi Valley" half the prince and no freeway noise."

I turn to my sweet friend, Jacqueline, and no beat missed she replies "location, location, location" and we melt, hysterical, howling amidst caskets and professional death sitters waiting for tips for reciting psalms in the night with newly dead, not yet welcome and ready for heaven.

And it goes on and on.

There are so many planning to come from far and near, so do come, and introduce yourself to the person next to you and share a story and a smile and do one good deed a day in Tony's memory and all will be well.

THE FUNERAL CAN ONLY BE 45-50 MINUTES LONG
SO, WE WILL HAVE TIME FOR ONLY A FEW SPEAKERS AT THE FUNERAL. WE WILL HAVE A MIC AT THE TENNIS CLUB AND ANYONE WHO CARES TO SHARE MORE STORIES
AT THAT TIME WILL BE WELCOME.

I hope that covers everyone.

My sweetheart has still not called, not shown up to take the dog for a ride in his convertible. He is so oddly absent while still with me, breathing the angels breath now and charming the gatekeepers. My god, how can we be without him? We now must do his work of goodness each and every one of us.

I picked up Rafaella from the top of the hill, as she struggled not to stumble heading down to Franklin for the bus today. And she told me she was Rafaella and she asked me who I was.
"You drive me down the hill. Who are you so nice person?"
"Tony, I am," I said. And I was, in his name.

See you Thursday, come early, there will be many of us.
love

FRIDAY, MARCH 21, 2008
RESTING RESTING BLESSED

Thank you for blessing Tony with your love and celebration.

If you were not with us in person yesterday—over 400 people strong— you were there in spirit—faces floated at me. Such joy and beauty and I come away from yesterday and into today with the knowledge that

T accomplished what he was after.

He made a place for himself in the world.
He made a positive impact.
He affected people's lives.

I woke to a garden full of flowers and a trickle of friends here during the day bearing Chinese donuts and receiving Hawaiian shirts for safekeeping. We are sitting Shiva here at the house at 7 every night thru Tuesday, food at 5, please come join us as we continue to process this transition, letting go of old habits and welcoming the new, somehow struggling to create new and stronger ways of being rather than sinking back into painful patterns that have taken their toll on all of us.

Such is growth, such is survival and what is necessary to flow with grace from one epoch to another.

I have pasted both my speech and my daughter, Sofie's, for you to read. I will continue to write as makes sense, if you'd like to hear of our progress and healing for a little time at least.

There are CD's of the ceremony available if anyone would like one. Please email me and let me know.

Blessings and thanks
s

MY WORDS FOR THE FUNERAL

Hello friends
If you have yet to meet the person sitting next to you
Please turn to them and catch their eye,
let them feel your hand on theirs.
Mark them as a sign upon your heart and upon your soul,
for they are the stuff of the community

to which we belong.
For we have traveled—certainly the last part—
on this road together,
and for this I am enormously grateful
and truly honored.
And you have more than my thanks.

I learned from my partner, my friend,
the man of my dreams and delight of my eyes,
I learned that such people as you exist.
I learned that there is goodness and hope,
there is yes instead of steady no.
I have learned that love shows itself in the strangest of places
and in the secret madness of familiarity,
and the arrogant contempt for time.

I have learned that loving is complex and fierce
and leaving and returning,
and steadily stubbornly every day saying yes,
and I am so endlessly sad that I must now cull and quantify the lessons
and loving learned in this part of my beautiful life,
with my beautiful man—
now, I build memory upon memory into the new beginning of the rest
of my days.
With our gorgeous and strong daughter
and whatever adventures we may encounter.

I should tell you, too, that in the last two months,
the months that we really thought his life was ending—only to be bushwhacked by hope—in those months of scotch and ice cream and hilarity and joy we found each other again and Tony found himself—because of all of you. He felt his worth, his life's work palpable in your love and expressions of support. My god what a gift—to know and feel your worth—and I know and feel he finally ingested that final masterstroke to his beauty.

Tony Shultz—my husband and companion of 27 years—was beauty, incarnate.
I drew pleasure and delight from his java chip ice cream to his two tone saddle shoes.
From the sports cars that never worked,
to the years of trails we traveled on faraway continents,
and on the journey of our spirits
…from the feel of his skin.
I have been honored to be his wife, his friend, his fellow traveler.

Juliet spoke of her Romeo:
"And when he shall die
take him and cut him up into little stars
for he shall make the face of heaven so bright
that all the world will be in love with night and
pay no more tribute to the garish sun."

I carry his heart. I carry it in my heart.

✳✳✳

WORDS FROM
Sofie Shultz

The past three months have been both terrifying and incredible. The news of my dad's illness was shocking and scary, but we all stood together to support each other. But I say it was incredible because of the things I felt compelled to say to my father. Things that normally I would not have said. I got to ask him what he wanted me to be, and where I should go. To ask him what I should do for him to be proud of me forever. He told me that whatever I did, as long as I wanted to do it and be it, and was happy, that he would be proud of me. With a shortened amount of life and the thought that your parents will live forever, urged me to tell him I'd miss him for the special things in my life that he wouldn't get to be here for: graduation, college, walking me down the aisle. Things I really wanted him to be there with me for. His response is one that will live forever with me: "I want to be there for you just as much as you want me to be there."

My dad lived with the finest things. He was a Jaguar man, my Disneyland dad.

Being home for the past few days has given me the chance to look around and examine the life he lived; just as he did. All the artifacts, the art, the music, the love that fills our house now shows the wonderful life he lived. It truly was a beautiful life.

I miss him. But he will never be gone. I know that he wanted to be here, to see me grow up, and so he will never leave my side.

He gave me strength, us strength, in our sorrow. And showed me that I am strong, even when I don't feel I am.

Thanks, dad. As my grandma Evie said, it's been a beautiful life.

SUNDAY, MARCH 23, 2008
RESURRECTION SUNDAY

...So, it's Easter and just down the boulevard at the Hollywood Bowl they are singing to raise the dead.

Our Shiva is continuing. Last night a beautiful mournful clarinet and friends and family and food and dying Easter eggs in the fountain and ricotta cheese cake and starting to cull the wilting flowers from the many, many bouquets and some departures.

My brother who stood as a tower next me as I started to list like Pisa having to say the first Kaddish.. and the Berkeley boys into men who are the true spirit of T more than any others and the once merely depressed P now morphed into a man of joy and science and spirit, investigating the soul and what gives us those spirits that make us who we are,

And changing the sheets on which T last slept...
finally,
with my women who knew just how to bless our marriage bed
with sage and soft voices and the release of spirit,
the light of comfort

and finally, a walk on the beach,
with family all together
and laughter in the living room
and our little house full of us all together
so much comfort, so much joy, so much fuel for the transition
too beautiful
too grateful
and Monday the Klezmer band plays
and Tuesday we finish up and take a walk around the block

and so we begin a anew.
thank you everyone for mourning with us,
my god we are so fortunate.

I go now to offer some pies to the kids at Covenant House on Easter Sunday
and then swim and return to pray.
Join us if you can,
s

And below are words from friend, Bob.
You need to read them—

In Honor of Tony Shultz
by Bob Tzudiker

We think of Tony as the personification of gentleness. But you would not feel that way if you were a wedge of cheese. Especially a soft cheese. Brie lived in fear of Tony.

I would always marvel at Tony's approach to a cutting board. His whole being became purposeful, he would flow toward that cheese, not with greed or gluttony, but with the same sense of purpose as a river flowing towards its own mouth. That's how Tony would flow toward that poor cheese.

Once he arrived at the cutting board, Tony would pick up the knife, but he used it as a shovel—gracefully, delicately, he'd carve off a spade full of that cheese. He had no respect for crackers; he'd inundate them, disappear them under a small mountain of cheese. And all of it would be gone in a second, at once both genteel and voracious.

Tony was serious about all his pleasures. Very serious. For all his many talents, pleasure was his true art. He made it profound, a form of worship.

One of the hard things about being alive is when you realize that something will never be again. It's such a peculiar feeling, and we all share it now— that sweet sting of appreciation of what will never be again. I will never again see Tony eat cheese. But that doesn't mean he can't still be my guru of appreciation. To Tony, a fine meal was brushed with immortality.

MONDAY, MARCH 24, 2008
KLEZMER UNDER THE STARS

Though Bob Dylan and Neil Young were more his style, last night cousin Betsy and friend Michael Hecht and their klezmer band played mournful melodies and sweet syncopations in the garden under the stars for our Tone. And more food, and more friends and Easter eggs for Isaiah right along with lilacs on the table and the sounds of davening and working women—and men—in the kitchen.

Making the food, cleaning the plates, doing the dishes, turning over the barbecue to my darling friend to cook in T's honor…sitting on low benches and soft green chairs and hearing SPACEBALLS play in the office where another gaggle of kids gathered for T in their way.

I can feel the shift now. T almost jetisoned(sp?) to the upper realms but lingering close enough to enjoy the party. What a glorious send off.

And now tonight, chili and Kaddish to come, and more friends and a quieter time, perhaps and maybe more music? Or poetry, or being together simply as we wend our way to tomorrow and our walk around the block ending Shiva and beginning the rest of our lives.

Come be with us if you can these last two nights. We need you to eat and laugh and enjoy the rich syrup of love oozing from every corner, refilling our little house with T's spirit.

How grateful I am to you all, for me, for Sof, for Tone

Sooon
sooooon
soooooooooon
we will return to our lives
we are winding down and gearing up.

We are preparing and we are prepared.
much love
s

AND SO IT GOES

...so many people
the back garden like a catering hall
and every night for seven nights
enough buzz and energy to light up the city of Manhattan
for a year or two.
And tonight, too,
another blast of beauty with the last night of Shiva and
the basketball boys showing up
and Ilene and Joy from GREASE days and
more food and more friends and more flowers

and more music
and then, we walked,

Sofie and I, me barefoot
she strolling on my arm,
we walked with Audrey the dog
in front of us
around the corner ending Shiva and back to life...
and as we rounded the corner Audrey (our dog)
began to snarl and bark at other dogs behind bars
and we rounded the other corner to head back and there was
the parking police ticketing everyone
everyone, everyone on the block

and much to do
and much plummeting from the earthly realms back to reality.

Tone is ready to jettison himself further upward
already gone there I bet,
not around to fix parking tickets and
barking dogs and piles of uneaten cookies
and flowers off their blooms.
And so we begin
Sof and I,
inch by inch, back in the world.

Thank you to everyone who has been in touch with us,
cards and smiles and songs and calls,
thank you for pausing to celebrate a life well lived,
thank you for sharing the joy of our lives together now.

We will see how we move forward,
a little at a time.
We have work to do and balance to be found
I will probably continue to not answer the phone or even check messages,
so please email me if you'd like to be in touch.

And if I am quiet for a while,

that is a good and necessary thing,
I have enough smoothed shoulders and kisses
and eyes of loving and sympathy for now to digest
and Sof will figure out how to mourn…inch by inch as
we have done thus far.

The Bloc will be back in a week or so.
I am doing a reading of Bounty of Lace,
my Israeli play about women's response to life in a war zone,
this week at a conference at Loyola Marymount.
I will prepare the New Play fest at school,
and Sof will go on a choir tour,
and we will see.

We will feel and touch and sink and rise as the breath comes and goes.

If you have a dish or a pot or a pan,
once filled with gorgeous gracious food for us all
please come by and pick it up.
I will leave everything at the top of the driveway and you can come anytime.

Much love
and thanks
from Tony and his family,
now changed and full of his heart
for all time.

WEDNESDAY, MARCH 26, 2008
…THE FIRST DAY OF THE REST OF MY LIFE

Odd.
Now hollow. Strange but simple.
A day of being a person.
Sof home, cuddling in with TV,
and Audrey.

Stillness.
Fingers and toes done, then back to work.
Strong in the house, the feeling of the energy soaked into the walls
and now faint.
We venture steps away here and there
but are drawn back.
Out of body,
out of my mind
xxoo
s

FRIDAY MARCH 28, 2008
HELLO OUT THERE

Hello out there
Shifting, shifting.
I can actually feel the energy shifting in the house
little by little.
The first memorial candle is out.
The flowers, so glorious in first blush, are starting to wilt,
and we are doing the little things.
Replacing the table cloth with a clean one and
moving the smaller table,
now enough for us two,
back to the center of the dining room
I once thought small and
now know to have been the scene
of the most expansive of celebrations.

The chicken barbecued on the grill
is burnt.
T did that.
And the trash cans, those too I pulled in by myself tonight
and new habits for Sof.
How to dine with mom? Her sweet desire to make me feel okay?

But she has not completed a full meal at the table since she hit her teen
years, so...the cup of tea after dinner, now with...Audrey.
Yes, that will be fine.

It is not crushing,
this readjustment,
it is odd and hollow at times
and in yoga class opening the heart chakra was a killer
but according to the Grief Recovery Handbook
which my friend Michael was quick with,
the true grief is with the unfinished conversation,
the doubt lingering,
the odd ripping of the fabric when unprepared.
Yes, there is all that
but not as much, yet, as one would have thought.

Have not read all the cards and
looked at all the pictures yet.
It is inch by inch,
but I did receive a card from the surgeon,
full of such sad compassion
..."still unclear what happened, but what is clear is that our hearts and
prayers are with you."
That is a Zen master struggling with his own heart.

Ah me.

So much love still around us,
but giving us space to take our steps
into the world,
seeing who we may be now that we have us
a cosmic partner.

I wonder if anyone is reading.
It feels quiet
quiet

with the feeling that there are scurrying footsteps
behind the scenes moving things around
rearranging the energy so that the next scene can play itself out.

Good night for now,
sleep well,
we shall see if the silk of sleep
is ready to soothe us for another night.

NEXT DAY
WHAT TO SAY

Not sure how to report in on the day to day
of living from here to there.
To report on the rewiring of the heart
and the way music finds its way underneath
the cellular structure of the heart.
And how strong I feel in the house and
how the strength drains away the
farther from the energy base that I go.

Not sure how to write about grief
and quiet and the sound of the wheels on
the road when NPR is off and
there is nothing but the sound
of the Audi, T's Audi,
car moving along the road.

The tasks of transition almost done,
death certificates sent out,
money on its way,
taxes being attended to,
and most closets cleaned.

And then taking up the tasks of
everyday.

Rewired.
That is probably the best way to describe this time.
A time of rewiring and shorting out.
and re-plugging and unsure about
where the unused wires are supposed to go.

Certain things are true.
Conversations are heard in a different light.
Talk of minor illness, the illness that is comforting somehow
as it defines our time of life,
that kind of illness seems welcomed by many
confused and unsure how to accept the next stage of life.
An old concern, different for me now.

There is a certainty about what connects.
Listening to the music and prayers in a Shabbat service
is like having my skin peeled,
in a weird ritual of relief kind of way.

There are new awarenesses about
spirit and slotting growth.

There is a quiet and a boring into the heart,
that is both painful and liberating I suppose.

There are still the details of loss to handle.
Choosing the plot,
wording the stone for my husband.
And moving from place to place to place

My turn pushing the wheel.
Omigod

WEDNESDAY, APRIL 16, 2008
SO IT'S BEEN A WEEK....

...Since I've written and was wondering

when I would get back to this
very public, very private display
of this very private and yet quite public event.

It has been a month now,
since he's gone and
new tragedies have started crowding the landscapes—
parents with strokes
children with cancer
and the flowers blooming anyway.

T told me he checked the blog to see how it was all going.
To see how he felt
and what was next and inside ourselves
and he is gone now
and I realize that this blog was his—
an expression of him and the way in which he
intersected with his world
and experience.

And I am not him,
I am what's left of a part of him.

My gash is more gaping perhaps than most
but as I inch along the snail-y trail of tears,
I move more and more from him
into myself and

so my words, revelations, abilities to share
discoveries to acknowledge become
more focused and more mine,
less, ours.

I am not sure of all the ways I will be me
separate from Tony,
it is all in the mix at the moment,

but it is figuring out the new voice that stops me from
flippantly reporting on internal shifts and
magic elixirs applied as in the Hogwarts infirmary—
poof! You have a new leg.

My new legs, arms, heart are not yet buds
only yet stumps, amputated—bloody, coagulating

and though I look down the hallway toward the light
I am still in the corridor looking backward and forward,
paralyzed by then, now and maybe and
the galloping, galloping as fast as I can.

All of this is to say,

Hello
I'm getting new,
and not sure who will come out the other end of this tunnel.

I just know that life is waiting between now and death.

Hello. I'm getting new. And you are too.

RECOGNITION
a one act play

SARAH AND JAKE, 50s, WATCH THE YOUNGER, SARI AND JACOB, 30s, MEET.

FIRST SECTION IS A RUSH OF EXCITEMENT.

     SARI
Omigod! I recognize you!

     JACOB
You do?

     SARI
I do.

     JACOB
How come?

     SARI
Aren't you?

     JACOB
You look so much like my…

     SARI
My god! You get it?

JACOB
You like that wine?

SARI
My mom told me I'd find someone like…

JACOB
A walk together. How about the boat basin?

SARI
I love the boat basin.

JACOB
How about some Chinese food and Central Park? Panda Express and Beaujolais. Sound good?

SARI
Perfect.

JACOB
And then tomorrow…

SARI
Maybe. I think. Yes, a movie would be good.

JACOB
A movie?

SARI
A walk across the park

JACOB
With bikes

SARI
At midnight

JACOB
You're nuts…

SARI
You're perfect.

JACOB
Will you…

SARI
I do.

JACOB
I do too.

SARI
I do. I now pronounce us. We are forever.

JACOB
Husband and wife.

> THEY EMBRACE AND BREATHE IN EACH OTHER'S ARMS. BEAT. THEY ARE MARRIED.
> RHYTHM CHANGES.
> THE HONEYMOON.

SARI
Oh man. I felt the earth move. I mean, didn't you feel the earth move? It's different. It's different now, isn't it? The earth moved. We're married. Being married. It's different.

JACOB
I'm tired. Let's dance.

SARI
Let's dance all the way to Paris…

JAKE
Where you woke up at 3 AM, looking over the rooftops of Paris and said,

    SARI, IN A PANIC REALIZES
    WHAT SHE HAS DONE

SARI
I can return all the wedding gifts. I can. I can simply call up my mother and tell her save all the cards and I will return the gifts. We don't need to go through with this. This has been a terrible mistake.

JACOB
C'mon! We're making memories!

SARI
I'm terrified.

JACOB
Look in your wedding ring?

SARI
What?

JACOB
In your wedding ring. Look at it. I wrote you a message.

SARI
(takes off her ring and reads it)
"Don't be frightened." That's what you wrote?

JACOB
Yep.

SARI
What the hell does that mean? That's not very encouraging.

JACOB
It's insurance. We're too broke for life insurance so I figure I'll give you some advice you can always count on. How's that?

SARI
It's weird. You're weird.

JACOB
I am your husband, forever. Even if you do return the gifts.

SARI
Can I borrow your toothbrush?

JACOB
It's in the dop kit.

SARI
I want to use it.

JACOB
Didn't you bring your own?

SARI
I want to use yours. Can I use yours?

JACOB
You can use mine.

SARI
Here, kiss me. Breathe into my mouth.

JACOB
I thought you wanted to go home?

SARI
I do. But kiss me first.

JACOB
Before you use my toothbrush? Or after?

SARI
Breathe into my mouth. I want your breath in my body. Can I sip your breath?

JACOB
How much did you smoke last night?

> AND THEY PLAY AND KISS. THEY BREAK
>
> SARAH ADDRESSES THE AUDIENCE AS THE YOUNGER COUPLE SPOONS IN BED.
>
> SARAH AND JAKE COME DOWN AND SIT AT A TABLE, REGALING FRIENDS (THE AUDIENCE) WITH THEIR STORY—A SET PIECE OF THEIR MARRIAGE.

SARAH
And we went on this amazing honeymoon. All through France and then across Spain and then down to Portugal

and to Morocco and all the time it's getting hotter and we're driving the Deux Cheveaux across the desert. And that got old...and we ended in some pit of dust with camels and guys with scimitars. Really—scimitars—

JAKE
Morocco, wow! It was great!

SARAH
If you like walking three feet behind your husband in the camel shit—in 300 degrees—and carrying the bundles on your head so the camel doesn't get overheated!

JAKE
...and there was that bride on the ferry. Do you remember? Covered from top to toe in henna. Designs...like on a sacred scroll maybe...or soft patterned acne scars...

SARAH
You shall take them as a sign upon your heart and upon your soul...

JAKE
...for frontlets between thine eyes...

SARAH
And it was fucking hot. So goddamn hot!

JAKE
It was gorgeous. What do you mean? What an amazing place. (He warms to the story.) Swiss chalets! In Morocco. All these French types had settled.

SARAH
You've heard of the French Foreign Legion? David Niven? He was nowhere to be seen.

JAKE
The French made these great settlements. And there we were. Top of the Rif Mountains and it was glorious. There were merchants on the side of the road.

SARAH
Rocks. They sold rocks. Honestly. Rock merchants and people would buy them. I mean tourists would… They would actually buy them…

JAKE
They were geodes.

SARAH
Some. Some were…but those were the ones next to the spitting monkeys. You took your life in your hands to go near those. The others were…

JAKE
Aw c'mon! Spitting monkeys…

SARAH
There were goddamn spitting monkeys… They perched on the overhangs and as tourists came to buy the ROCKS.

JAKE
Geodes…

SARAH 1
…the monkeys would hiss and jump on their backs! Like God damn Wizard of the Oz, "and your little dog too!"

JAKE
It wasn't that bad.

SARAH
No. No. It wasn't. I have a bad attitude.

JAKE
You did, you do, and I try to make it better.

SARAH
Yes! Yes, you did! You do… Oh, don't get your feelings hurt. I apologize.

JAKE
I'm trying to tell a story here…

SARAH
Yes, yes. I apologize, my darling.

SATISFIED, HE CONTINUES

JAKE
So, we had been on the road about 6 weeks by then, and we had braved the beauties of Spain and the terror of handing our passports over into the hands of a crowd of turbaned fellows at the border.

SARAH
Where he was offered two camels and a jug of wine as a trade for me, I might add…

JAKE
I didn't take it.

SARAH
My hero.

JAKE
She was having a rough trip.

SARAH
It was August. The Sahara desert. We were driving a Deux Cheveaux.. the putt-putt French car, and he had the top of it rolled back…

JAKE
To get a little sun…

SARAH
I say again, it was August in the Sahara desert. And I had watched our passports disappear into a hole in a concrete building while he negotiated with a Bedouin about how many camels I was worth.

JAKE
Oh come on. The passports came back…

SHE LOOKS AT HIM

JAKE
And I didn't sell you.

SARAH
Thanks, darling.

JAKE
Maybe that was a mistake.

SARAH
And then you backed over those sacred leaves in that sacred town while they were getting ready for their feast day.

JAKE
That WAS a mistake…

SARAH
And we had to beat it out of town, pursued by buzzy motorbikes manned with boys who I did NOT go to Hebrew school with…

JAKE

She was not calm. She was not enjoying the adventure.

SARAH

And we finally arrived in this Berber village where he promised me we could stay at a beautiful spot—The Beau Sejour.

JAKE

How was I to know it was full of bug spray and a cockeyed drugged-out rocker in hiding?

SARAH

He drooled. The guy who ran the hotel. He actually drooled…and leered…

JAKE

…so I took you down for some kebabs to cool you out…

SARAH

And we sat down at a little café and I picked up a skewer to eat a kabob and…it flew away! Skewer covered with flies. It flew away…

JAKE

Just a couple of…

SARAH

And I said to him…

SARI ROLLS OUT OF BED
AND SPEAKS FIRMLY

SARI

Jacob, I'm going to Casablanca. By bus. I will go to Casablanca and get a plane home and you finish the trip. I can't take this anymore. I need to get out of here.

JAKE
And I said…

>JACOB SITS UP TO TALK TO HER.

JACOB
Aw c'mon Sarah. C'mon. let's take a walk. Calm down. It'll be okay.

>JAKE AND SARAH WATCH AS JACOB AND SARI MOVE TO THE MOUNTAIN AREA.

SARAH
And he walks me across the street avoiding the camels and the leering tribesmen and…

JAKE
It was a holy mountain.

JACOB
Look! There's a big red star there. C'mon, let's walk up. We'll sit. We'll talk. We'll look at the view.

SARAH
And we began to climb up and we look out at a green soccer field across the way and the volcanic rock is…

SARI
…It's all crevice-y and hard.

JACOB
Lava rock! Isn't that cool?

SARI
You're talking to me.

JACOB
I'm talking you off the ledge.

SARAH
You think you're making headway.

JAKE
And I am making headway…

SARAH INTERJECTS

SARAH
…I AM being charmed, because he is charming, always has been charming.

JAKE
And I was trying hard and I notice…

SARAH
There's this guy who's run up to the top of the hill, and he disappeared for a couple of minutes and then he just trots down..

JAKE
But I keep talking to you, keep trying to calm you down…

SARI
Uh—Jake—there's another guy going up to that other part of the mountain. Over there. See. I think—look, he's disappearing for a minute and he's trotting back down, fiddling with his belt.

JACOB
Look, Sarah, I'm talking to you here…

SARI
But look! There's someone else…

>SARAH NARRATES AS THE YOUNGER SARI DOES THE ACTION

SARAH
…and then I look down to keep my focus, save my marriage, listen to my wise new husband. I look to my feet and I notice that there seems to be…

SARI
Shit?

JAKE
Aw shit! There was shit everywhere!

SARAH
I look around and all around us on the ground, tucked into crevices, every corner, every air pocket—there was human…

SARI
Shit! Everywhere!

JAKE
Not everywhere!

SARI
Shit!

JAKE
Ok, ok…shit…everywhere…

SARI
We are sitting and sorting out our marriage on Shit Mountain, in the middle of the public bathroom for the bus station... For Chrissakes, Jacob...

JAKE
How was I supposed to know?

JACOB
In trouble here...

SARI
Unbelievable. Omigod!! I'm losing it! I'm hyperventilating!

AND SHE IS.

JACOB
So come on. I'll get you down. I'll find somewhere beautiful, you'll see.

SARAH
To your credit or the ecumenical prayers to Allah...you got me down. By this time I am apoplectic and catatonic at the same time.

JAKE
And I get you to this beautiful French chalet in the woods. It...

SARI(weeping)
Oh! It's beautiful!

SARAH
It was like an apparition, it was so beautiful, and I hobble out of the car, drag my pathetic self to the front door, weeping, puddle, and the door swings back and...

JACOB
Voila!

SARAH
Gleaming like the shining city on the hill…

SARI
White tablecloths and lamb chops on perfect plates and *petit pois* and *haricot verts* and I…CAN'T STOP CRYING!

SHE WAILS.

JACOB
You're crying harder… Why are you…

SARI
I can't stop, actually.

JACOB
I'll get us a room for the night in this beautiful French Swiss chalet place. Okay? Calm down. Calm down… Oh, no rooms available, Madame?

SARI
No rooms available, Madame? (She wails again.) Are you sure?

SARAH
I was weeping and weeping!

SARI
(Weeps harder, on cue)
Waaahhhhh!

JACOB, NOT KNOWING WHAT TO DO, GIVES HIS WIFE A GLASS OF WINE. HE TAKES IT FROM THE SMALL CAFÉ TABLE WHERE SARAH AND JAKE ARE SITTING.

JACOB
Beaujolais! Drink up!

   SARI TAKES WINE AND
   CRIES ALL THE HARDER

SARI
I wanna go home!

JAKE
Finally the Madame took pity on us, and she made me help her take some old beds out of a storeroom and we set ourselves up in there and, finally, blessedly, thank god. We took a shower and went to bed, drunk on good red wine…

JACOB
Compliments of Madame.

   SARI SMILES WEAKLY AT
   HIM AS HE TUCKS HER IN
   AND THEY SETTLE IN BED.

SARAH
The next day was the first time you left me. Well, not exactly…

SARI
…on our honeymoon in a Swiss chalet in the Moroccan countryside? You're going hiking?

JACOB
I'm taking a walk. I need a break. You are in no shape.

SARI
You going hiking? In the middle of the spitting monkeys and the cockeyed drug dealers and the Shit Mountains?

AND HE LEAVES HER.

SARAH
...and I lay in bed and waited...'til late at night.

JACOB TIPTOES BACK IN

JACOB
Hi, Sarah. Sleeping?
SHE DOESN'T SPEAK TO HIM

C'mon. I wasn't gone so long.

SARI
All day. I waited and waited and then it was dusk and then it was night. And I ate my lamb chops alone and went to bed and...what time is it?

JACOB
About 11...

SARAH
And you slept and the next day you got up and went hiking again...

SARI
Jake, you're leaving me alone here. All by myself. I'm afraid.

JACOB
No you're not. You'll be fine, Sarah. You'll survive just fine. I gotta go. I just gotta go.

SARAH
And I wanted so much to make it better. I searched through our luggage and found two pair of jeans and

managed to get the Deux Cheveaux started and went to the rock dealers and traded the jeans for two beautiful geodes—rocks—and I knew you would love them, right… and I thought I have saved our marriage!

JACOB
You were ripped off!

SARAH
You were furious!

JAKE
But we sat on the porch of the chalet. We just sat quietly.

SARAH
So you could calm down.

JAKE
And I looked around us and the sunset, the end of the day, was so very beautiful. (He takes a small beat.)

JACOB
I know it will be okay. Whatever happens.

JAKE
Next morning we got back into the Deux Cheveaux…

SARAH
Thank God you didn't leave me there. Man…

JAKE
And we called a truce. Remember? It was beautiful… We came out of the Ring Road around the little village and as we left the town the trees got denser and you were just about to say something about…

SARAH
We were in uncharted territory, Jake. I was scared. OK, I admit it.

JAKE
...and we rounded a corner and I cut the engine. Remember? And the little car started to move down the hill silently—wheeeee. We just let ourselves trust the hill.

It was truly grand. And out of nowhere we heard the gentle sound of hoof beats and the soft tinkle of jingle bells. Next to us, happily pacing our descent, was a handsome old palomino. He was trotting companionably, glancing into our window, tossing his head now and then, helping us sail down the hill in the early morning. You might say he was responsible for us making it through the rest of our honeymoon—and our marriage.

When things get tough, Sarah, think of that old horse clip-clopping along, giving us a nudge forward, helping us appreciate how good it is to trust the hill.

SARAH
After we went to Limoges, to get our wedding china, or maybe before— before, I think, we drove to a little town near there. Remember that? Oradur Sur Glane. It was in the Harvard Let's-Go Guide. We drove up in the Deux Cheveaux, putt-putting up the hill. There was no one there. An old stonewall in front of us, and just as we pulled up a pigeon let go with load right on our windshield.

JAKE
I had just washed that car...

SARAH
But there was a sign there: *Silence. Souviens Toi.* Hush. Remember?

JAKE

Hush. I remember.

SARAH

We moved ahead on the path of the old town silently. As directed. The entire village had been torched and left for dead. It was eerie and full of shadows. The empty patisserie. The bicycle shop with the frame of the racer dangling from the wall. Life interrupted in the middle of living, Jake.

JAKE

It happens, Sarah darling.

SARAH

I heard all those ghosts talk to me. Felt their hands brush me gently. Stroking me, making me feel better somehow. Telling me to remember, but somehow—the reminders were to live, not to die. There was work to be done still, this living still, somehow.

JAKE

Yes. It's what we do. What we say.

SARAH

But I miss you so terribly. I told you that night. When we knew you were sick. I reached across the table. I held your fingers, just the tops of them, and the crooked one that bent around the corner.

JAKE

Cut in the ceramics studio at Berkeley. Thank God, it kept me out of the draft.

SARAH

And I said to you, I said it.

SARI
I will miss you so terribly.

SARAH
And you just looked at me with your sad sweet eyes. But your sadness was for me, though. I thought that was so odd. Like you were already gone.

> **LIGHTS CHANGE AND JAKE IS NOW BACKLIT**

JAKE
A few months ago. When I was still there. On your side of the fence. And we hadn't started this phase of our relationship. This talking across time. We looked at each other one night, just after we found out...

SARAH
We were really afraid. We both knew. We were shy around it. Like maybe we shouldn't let it know we knew it was with us—fear. But then, what did we have to lose except what we lost anyway. So you say to me...

JACOB
"I'm afraid, Sarah. Are you afraid?"

SARI
"Yes, are you afraid?"

JACOB
"Yep." (Beat. Silence) "I just said I was afraid."

> BEAT. BEAT.

SARI
"Oh, right. Sorry."

JACOB
"So, what are we afraid of? Do we know?"

SARAH
"Says you, 'just-the-facts,' man."

SARI
"Yep, I say, I have a really long list…"

SARAH
…and I listed at least 27 things, and maybe then more. It was a clattery rattle in our little living room and you said…

JACOB
Wow! You have a really long list. Mine is shorter."

SARI
"But you're scared-er, right?"

JACOB
"Right."

SARAH
We looked around to see if fear heard.

JACOB
Fuck it. Who cares? You're prepared.

> BEAT. JAKE EXTENDS HIS HAND TO HER AND TAPS HER WEDDING RING WITH ONE FINGER.

JACOB
"Don't be frightened."
"Okay, let's go to bed. Okay?"

SARAH
You said to me…

SARI
"Okay."

SARAH
I answered.
And we did and we were still scared and
we still slept thru the night and
we still woke up and then

JAKE
It was a beautiful Sunday morning

SARAH
and we were still afraid.

JAKE
We were still there.
And we got another day of joy.

SARAH
Afraid or not.

JAKE
And you're still there.

SARI
And I'm still here. Oh, Jake.

JACOB
Remember Paris? Remember my breath in your lungs.

> HE COMES CLOSE TO HER
> AND KISSES HER ON THE
> FOREHEAD WITH A SIGH.

> SHE TAKES A DEEP BREATH.
> HE WALKS AWAY AND
> TURNS BACK TO HER.

JAKE
Talk to you tomorrow, love.

END OF PLAY

CARLA TELLS US WHAT HAPPENED IN THE BLUE BEDROOM
a monologue

CARLA, A WOMAN IN HER 50S, SITS QUIETLY IN HER SWING ON THE PORCH. SHE TAKES A SWIG OF TEA. SHE LOOKS UP AND SPEAKS SIMPLY.

CARLA

Houses are sentimental.

Nothing oozing from corners except memory and sound.

Nothing waiting in the closets

or under the beds except

the dust of years lived together

and creaky springs that got lazy

after too many attempts at sex when

it didn't matter much anymore.

And the old tennis balls from the dog,

chewed over and over and now not even buoyant, just left.

Like a widow, rolling against pillows that used

to hold her lover,

who became her husband, who became her friend,

then her companion, then her other lung and

the weight on her heart,

'til he curled peacefully to his side one night,

when I slept fitfully, for the first time

in so many months, in the next room.

Only to allow him rest. To allow us both a little rest.

"You're on your own," I said that to him.

"You're on your own!" Furious,

when he downed the last handful of pills.

"They aren't in the bottle, Jim. They're not in the bottles. All these

pills, all white, all powder, all different. How can you figure?"

"We'll sort them in the morning," he said to me.

"We'll sort them."

But he didn't. He wouldn't. I got out a magnifying glass.

A big one. I told him right then.

Carla Tells Us What Happened in the Blue Bedroom

"Now, let's sort it now!" Furious. Losing.

He flicked his hand at me. The one with the bent finger,

He took what he wanted and lay back

against the puffed pillows.

A fluffy bed I made for him.

Ridiculous. The things you do for comfort.

I lay down next to him. Watching him.

He startled at my eyes, demanding he be present.

watching his breath, holding him here on the planet.

So I gave in.

"You're on your own,"

I said to him and went to the room across the hall.

He breathed a sigh of relief as I passed through

the hallway.

"I'll hear him. I'll know if he needs me."

He didn't need me.

He wanted to be gone,

to be done, and so,

gently he turned to his side and

closed his beautiful eyes and slipped off.

A blessed death, they say, going that way.

A blessed death with little more suffering to endure,
That a blessing to be sure.

The police when they came—

Officer Jimmy and Officer Carl.

Young, so young and stiff.

They looked at me. Suspicious,

"The pills, ma'am?" they asked.

"And the magnifying glass, ma'am,?"

Looking at the plastic bag, the white box, the dirty glass on the

dresser.

They asked me. They looked hard.

They were ready to unroll the yellow tape and make the house a

crime scene,

But my wailing, I suppose. My wailing, my chant,

"Omigod, omigod…"

 It's all that would come,

"A cliché," that was all I could think of. "Omigod!" Comical. No

poetry there.

I think it scared those little police boys,

none with wives yet, none with lives or history.

They left. They slunk off. Peeling back their white plastic gloves and

their grim eyes.

We loaded him beautiful on a gurney, with flowers and

a homemade quilt, and he was gone. Off to dust.

But the sentimental house,

the empty house with silent dust and empty corners,

The silent house oozes him—

And us—

And then,

And now, and I sleep and I wonder.

I just wonder if there will be breath here again.

A wind to push us to the next place,

Silent and possible.

Sunlight bruising death every day I'm left.

SHE TAKES A SIP.

Tea's cold. That's what happens.

SHE GETS UP THEN SITS BACK DOWN HOLDING THE MUG IN HER HAND. PUSHING THE CHAIR SLOWLY BACK AND FORTH WITH HER FEET. WAITING. LIGHTS FADE.

END OF PLAY

WHEN THEY GO AND YOU DO NOT

WE HEAR BUDDY HOLLY'S "THIS'LL BE THE DAY THAT I DIE" PLAYING. WENDY, A WOMAN IN HER FIFTIES, ENTERS WITH A LARGE PILE OF CLOTHES. SHE DUMPS THEM DOWNSTAGE AND SORTS HALF INTO ONE BOX AND HALF INTO THE OTHER. SHE REMOVES A LARGE MAN'S SHIRT AND HAT FROM THE SECOND BOX AND PUTS THEM ON OVER HER CLOTHES. SHE BECOMES EVAN.

WENDY

I believe in marriage. I do. I always knew I would get married and have a family.

And get a job. Somehow, manage to shoulder the white man's burden—

Hunter gatherer. All that crap. There are pluses along with the minuses. I mean there are the goddamn bills but it's a thrill when you sell a fucking car or a fleet of cars and you pocket a check for 20 thou and take the family to the beach for ten days and not have to sweat it. You just go back and do it again. Assume the mantle. I signed up for it. I get it. I got it. And I took it.

No matter how seductive pleasing a wife might be, there are still certain things, certain decisions that remain mine alone to make.

My wife has an agenda. Of course. Why not? I bought into it. She wants things her way, always did, always will. She loves me! Always did, always will. Told me all my faults, and I never went away. How to live my life, and I never went away. How to earn my living and spend it, and I never went away. Pushed and shoved and did everything she could, but I never went away. I was there, like a fact. It was great. I am her husband, forever. A matter of principle.

But, there comes a time. There came a time when my body got sick. My mother at the end of her life had sighed and said to me, "It's been a wonderful life, Evan" and I was so impressed with that. And I decided then and there that I would live my life every day to be able to say that and mean it. when my time arrived. I did that. And I was fine with that. I knew what was next and so did my wife.

But…she had to "handle" it.
Pray to the Chiclet God or whatever guru she was into at the particular time to make it go her way.

Still, that morning when she suggested we drive straight to the beach and drive up the coast and forget about going to the hospital, I smiled and we went to the hospital. I got on the operating table. I didn't look at her when they put the needle in my back, because I knew, I knew they were doing it wrong. Hell, I had set it up. And I didn't look at her, because she would know that I knew and she was watching like a hawk, her love an iron maiden around my planned escape.

When the surgeon went out to tell her that I was escaping, my blood pressure barely there, my heart beat waning—"I'm sorry, we don't know what's happening," he said to her—I can just see her eyes clicking and the steam coming out of her ears! And I think, yes, I think she even had ghost partners, by her side—her dead friends, that she was always seeing in woodland animals, chipmunks and squirrels…yes, a squirrel!

And her gay friend who really loved her but had already crossed over, he was there somehow when I was trying to escape and I swear he melted into his fucking squirrel persona and was chattering and skittering all over the courtyard screeching "He's getting away, Wendy! He's getting away!"

And my soul was rising higher and higher.
And I was almost there, just on the edge, seeing the light and ready to explode to the next life and I'll be goddamned if I didn't hear her chanting prayer,
"Not yet, you fucker! Don't you go yet!"
And just like that! You know what it's like. You lose concentration and then you're sunk and—thwack, I was slam back into my body and lying on that gurney while they continued all that slicing and peeling. Christ!

This was not on the agenda. Not MY agenda anyway.
When they rolled me up from the operating room to Intensive Care and I saw her there, sheepish and peering over at me and the three million fucking tubes in my body, I sat up. Actually lifted my sorry body to its full height like the ghoul I was planning to become, and screamed at her,
"God damn you Wendy. You got me back. Now what?"
And she knew. She knew I knew what she had done.

But I was a good man. A good husband and partner and I came back. And sat thru the days in the hospital where the jerks gave me the wrong meds and I saw a large Black man make peace in the Middle East and I was sure they were plotting to fire the cute little nurse that was washing me down every day. And I even went nuts for a few days there at the end until she sat with me. My Wendy. And held my hand and looked deep deep behind my eyes as only she could do and she gave in, her tears floating her yes right to the drip, drip, drip of my waiting heart. Waiting for that salve to soak it, and give me permission to do what I had in mind all along.

OK, I had to go through a little more to make it okay. We had to figure it out together before I could slip away. But that's a marriage after all. That's what a marriage is. A handshake, a bargain. And you do what you have to do, until your partner gets on board. So, I waited a little longer. But I did what needed to be done. We did what we had to do. That's love. I recommend it.

> LIGHTS CHANGE.
> WENDY EXPLODES INTO ACCUSATION AT A REMEMBERED MEMORY.

WENDY

"You're on your own!" I said that to him.
"You're on your own!" Furious!
And he downed the last handful of pills.
"They aren't in the bottle, Evan! They're not in the bottles! All these pills. All white. All powder, all different. How can you figure?"
"We'll sort them in the morning," he said to me. "We'll sort them."
But he didn't. He wouldn't.
I got out a magnifying glass. A big one. I told him right then.
"Now! Let's sort them now!" Furious. Losing.
"You're on your own!" I said to him.
"You're on your own," his eyes said to me.

> WENDY BACKS AWAY FROM THE MEMORY AND HEADS BACK TO THE BED. SHE DIVES UNDER THE COVERS. SHE HOLDS THEM TIGHT OVER HER EARS. COLLAGE OF VOICES IN HER DREAMS. SOUND OF CROWD OF

                    PEOPLE CHATTING,
                    MILLING,

FRIENDS/DIFFERENT VOICES (VO)
1: OY... I'M SO SORRY, WENDY DARLING! So young!

2: Call me anytime...but then, the kids and Joe and I are really are SO busy... and there are so MANY of us around the table.... I know another widow! I'll invite you both to dinner!

3: You had a long time. You're still young! And, well.... you didn't really get along that great anyway.

4: Here honey, lemme give you another hug. You'll be sleeping alone... after 27 years.

5: Lemme hug you again, sweetheart! HERE! GIMME A HUG HONEY....

                    WENDY SITS UP. ADDRESSES
                    THE AUDIENCE.

WENDY
When Evan died, seven months ago now, there were so many people trying to touch me. Pet me. Like kissing a Torah. Like if they touched my body, a totem, they would be blessed.

                    SHE PRESSES THE ANSWER-
                    ING MACHINE BUTTON. WE
                    HEAR EVAN'S VOICE:

EVAN(VO)
Hi, this is Evan and Wendy. Or actually Evan for Wendy. Well, it's us. You get the picture. Will you leave a message? Thanks.

                    WENDY CLICKS OFF THE
                    MACHINE. A GUILTY PLEA-
                    SURE

WENDY

On our honeymoon, mine and Evan's, after we went to Limoges, to get our wedding china, or maybe before. Before I think, we drove to a little town near there, Oradur Sur Glane. The entire town had been torched by the Nazi's and left for dead. So eerie, full of shadows. Life interrupted in the middle of living. There was a sign there: Silence. Souviens Toi. Hush—remember! But it wasn't quiet there at all. All those ghosts chattering, screaming, "Live Goddamit! Somehow live because we didn't. Be alive. Somehow still."

SHE CROSSES CENTER, FRANTIC.

I miss him so terribly. I told him I would that night. When we knew he was sick. I reached across the table. I held his fingers, just the tops of them, and the crooked one that bent around the corner.

And I said to him. I will miss you so terribly. We were really afraid when we heard the news, felt fear nudge its way between us—just for spite. But what did we have to lose except what we were losing anyway?
"I'm afraid, Wendy. Are you afraid?" Evan says to me.
"Yes, are you afraid?"
"Yes, Wendy, I just said I was afraid."
"Oh, right. sorry."
"So, what are we afraid of, do we know?" says Evan, ever the analyst.
"Yep, I say, I have a really long list—"
...and I rattle off a list of at least 27 things, each of them clanking noisy against the living room floor.
"Wow, he says, you have a really long list. Mine is shorter."
"But you're scared-er, right?"
"Right".
We look around to see if fear heard.
"Fuck it. Who cares?" Evan says to me.

"You're prepared." I look at him.
"Let's just go to bed like normal, okay?"
And we do and we are still scared and we sleep through that night and we wake up together the next mornings and many more mornings, like a game of chicken.

LIGHTS CHANGE.

The sunlight from the French windows is strong, refracted. I am lying on the bed next to Evan and I look up and see his soul floating on the ceiling, He is eyeing me, and obedient, comme d'habitude, my soul flies right up there next to his. Where it belongs. Where it has always been.

The rest of me, naked, slips back between the sheets, next to his still body, lifts his tee-shirt and places my belly, my breasts against his smooth chest, just not quite rubber. And just like that, he gives me a celestial shove from above! "Wake up and smell the coffee, babe, there's only one seat on this rocket ship. You're on your own."

The police when they come, Officer Jimmy and Officer Carl. Young, so young and stiff. They look at me. Suspicious.
"The pills, ma'am?" they say.
"And the magnifying glass, ma'am?" they ask.
They look at the plastic bag, the white box, the dirty glass on the dresser. They ask me. They look hard. They're ready to unroll the yellow tape and make the house a crime scene.

I think it scared them, these little police boys, none with wives yet, none with lives, or history. They leave. They slink off. Peeling back their white plastic gloves and their grim faces. And we load him beautiful on a gurney, with flowers and a homemade quilt, and he is gone. Off to dust.

SHE WATCHES AS THEY
ROLL HIM AWAY.

WHAT MATTERS: A WIDOWS LAMENT
WHAT MATTERS
is that I am here, I suppose
and he is not.
What matters is that porosity affects possibility.
That is, the membrane between life and death
bounces me back at life fiercely
not letting me join the club
excluding me.

What matters is hard to know when
half your soul has slipped like jello through the grate
though you are unwelcome to follow.

What matters is not that he is dead,
but that I am alive.

And what matters is elusive
as I float and flounder
through the months
toward purpose again
and song.

                        THE PHONE RINGS. THE
                        MACHINE PICKS UP.

                EVAN (VO)
Hi, this is Evan and Wendy. Or actually Evan for Wendy....

                        WENDY PICKS UP THE
                        PHONE.

                WENDY
Hello... Oh. No, he's not here. The dog? Ellie? Yes... the dog, my dog. I know you have HIS name but HE isn't here and he won't be back. No. No. Dead. He's dead. Yes, me too. Dead maybe about 7 months now. What's wrong with the dog?

ELLIE (VO)

Ah OOOOOOOOOO

WENDY

Oh my god. Is that Ellie? Well, can't you give her the rescue remedy or.

ELLIE (VO)

Ah OooooOOOOOOO

WENDY

Yes. Yes. I HEAR HER. Okay. Well, I know its been a week but, well, its so sunny today.

ELLIE (VO)

Ah oooOOoooOooOOO

WENDY

I do know we live in California and it's always sunny here!! There's nothing but sunshine here!! It's so fucking CHEERY! NO! Do NOT put her back on the plane. She was sent back TO me. (beat) SPF 30 doesn't help.

ELLIE (VO)

Ah ooooOOOOOOO!!

WENDY

I'll get there! Well, as soon as I can find a parasol…

ELLIE(VO)

Ah oooo

SHE SLAMS DOWN THE PHONE.

WENDY

What is the use of grief?

Thomas Jefferson asked that question.
He handled everything!
The creation of a great country,
building of a great house,
a swell time in Paris with his daughter.
And the loss of his wife.
His dear wife. So young.
And he promised her on her deathbed to never marry again.

Three weeks he never left his rooms.
And then he roamed the countryside like a mad man on horseback
And it's said that the spirit of his beautiful wife rode with him.
A ghost on his shoulder,
Draping her love over his back as he moved.
Kept himself moving, moving.
Until he could feel himself again and take up his life.

They had had six children and only three survived.
He was to lose another one before the end of his life
And he actually loved again…before Sally Hemmings…
A totally inappropriate Mrs. Cosgrove. A British lady he met in France.
They had a magical month together in France
And her departure sent him into such despair as to question.

Now what is the use of grief?
He even wrote a dialogue with himself.
Head and heart.
Balancing, digging, asking himself,
"I have roamed and shaped the world but
how am I to survive this
enormous emptiness that threatens
to swallow me whole no matter
what intellect I apply to it?, says he.
What is the use of grief?

> DECISION TO GET OUT OF
> THE HOUSE. SHE DRESSES
> AS SHE SPEAKS.

I bought a gym membership. Last week? When was it? Haven't been going out much these days. Body is still alive. Resilient, strong, malleable, willing. The muscles may have atrophied. I may need a physical therapy stun gun but there is still my heart, the thing beating inside. The thing that I still feel. My heart still pumps. Gushes. Thumpity thump thump. Thumpity thump thump. That is my heart.

> SHE STARTS TO JOG IN
> PLACE

Evan. His fingers head to the place on his neck where he is constantly checking his racing heart. (she sings)
"Oh, this'll be the day, oh ho ho.
This'll be the day, oh ho ho
This'll be the day hay hay
That I die."
That is Evan's heart.

I bought this bed as a gift for Evan. We slept in it from Romeo and Juliet all the way through Archie and Edith. This bed still holds my heart.

> THE BED CALLS HER TO IT
> AND SHE CANNOT RESIST.

I will go to the gym tomorrow. Really. Tomorrow. I will go to the gym.

> LIGHTS CHANGE AND SHE
> IS ASLEEP. THE SOUND OF
> THE SPRINKLERS WAKE
> HER

Why do I hear the water gush
from the sprinklers in the garden?
Thumpity thumpity thump!
Thumpity thump thump!

> GRABS HER CHEST. SHE
> CRADLES HER ARMS.

Ah! My heart is broken.
I have a broken heart.
My mother lost in a mental hospital
struggling to communicate from her deep well
with me on the other end of a bad pay phone.
"My heart is broken
I have a broken heart", she said that.
She ended up there when her husband died.
She survived four.

> SOUND OF WATER GUSHING
> IN THE GARDEN

Why is the damn water
gushing in the damn garden?
What matters is that he is dead
And I am not.
What matters is that I cannot touch my body
Without the memory of our years seeping.
Why is that damn water rushing in the garden?
My heart is broken.
I have a broken heart.
My heart is broken.
I have a broken heart.

> SHE COLLAPSES IN A CHAIR
> WHERE SHE SLEEPS THE
> NIGHT.
> LIGHTS CHANGE.
> MORNING

EVAN (VO)
Hi! This is Evan and Wendy. Or actually Evan for Wendy. Well, it's us. You get the picture. Will you leave a message? Thanks.

WENDY
They're calling about my dog again. OK. I made the choice to abandon her. Yes. We're all moving on and she's the victim. The dog went to live with cousins but she howled all the time. I can't bear to hear her howl all the time! She's the only one in this whole damn life thing that tells the truth!

> WENDY GATHERS HERSELF AND DIALS THE PHONE.

WENDY
UH.. hi there.. yes.. It's Wendy… uh… yes, the one with the dead husband. Wendy.. yes, and the dog. I know you tried to call. I can't come to the airport now. Today. I can't.. Well, I've bought a gym membership.

ELLIE (VO)
AH OOOOOOOO.

WENDY
Why did you bring her to the phone? I know what she sounds like. She sounds like ME!

> SHE SLAMS THE PHONE DOWN. IT RINGS AGAIN. THE MACHINE ANSWERS.

EVAN (VO)
Hi, this is Evan and Wendy. or Evan for Wendy…

WENDY (on the phone)
Hi! I apologize. I just…. They put her in quarantine!?

Why quarantine…well, she didn't fly because I told you not to…and so they put her in quarantine for a month? Oh, You're taking care of the situation, eh? I'm an unfit parent? An incapacitated parent? I KNOW I have to get it together. I told you I have bought a gym membership! My… heart.. is..! Calm? I am calm! I am nothing if not goddam fucking CALM! What? You'll keep her? Yes? So don't get too attached. She's had a major loss. Yes. Thank you, I appreciate you taking care of her. For now. Just for now. I have some work to do.

LIGHTS CHANGE.
BACK AT THE GYM

WENDY

I go to the gym.
Everyday.
I do sit ups
I crush the top of my stomach
as the ab machine says "pull me
pull me
pull me again you fucker.."
and I sit up again
and I pump more again
and I keep going because if I do not
I will die.

I step up and try to find center
and I falter and I step up and I hear
"now we will recite the kaddish for the dead".
And my body lists to the right like the leaning Tower of Pisa.

And I hear
"now we will recite the kaddish for the dead"
and I step up and I step up
and there are arms around me
and I step up and I step up
and there are hands in front of me

though I am standing alone
and I step up and I step up
and I step up and I step over
and I bypass the pit!
And I know
I will not fall there today.

PHONE RINGS.

EVAN (VO)
Hi, this is Evan and Wendy. Or actually Evan for Wendy. Well, its us. You get the picture. Will you leave a message? Thanks.

AND AGAIN

Hi, this is Evan and Wendy. Or actually Evan for Wendy. Well, it's us. You get the picture. Will you leave a message? Thanks.

> SHE ALMOST PUNCHES THE ERASE BUTTON BUT JUST PUNCHES THE MACHINE OFF.

WENDY
I wake up really early lately.
I go to the gym and do not fall into the pit.
It's remarkable really.
I go to the Astro Diner and have coffee.
At dawn. I watch the sun come up through the LA smog creeping on little cat feet and giant work boots
I head home and make the bed.
I sold the car last week.
Donated his record albums.
His drums went to the Professional Drum Shop.
Gave the guitar away… but kept the case.
I take a trip up north.

                              LIGHTS CHANGE.
A DREAM
On the beach at Big Sur
After the hoopla of friends
And cushion of memories
I come face to face with the stone doorway
And there I wade in the water
finally for now
and send the white ash to white foam
water streaming from the sky
as above so below
And committing to memory the
life I had loved
the luxury of coupling and complaint
I cross the threshold
draping fear on a nearby rock
and enter the future forever.
blessings. be upon you
and so it is.

                              WENDY RETURNS HOME.

The rain lashes the state from North to South.
I drive back to LA and watch the storm recede off the coast.
When I get back there is a gentle true blue sky
No punishing sun for a change.
I come back home
Look at my bed and see the clocks wrong
And the microwave flashing
And the timers on the lamplights confused

                              SHE MOVES TO THE
                              ANSWERING MACHINE

And Evan's voice is no longer there.

                              SHE PRESSES THE BUTTON
                              AND WE HEAR A LONG HISS.

WENDY HAS A SMOOTHIE
AT THE GYM BAR.

WENDY

It's been three months at the gym. A year since Evan's gone. I am at the gym a lot. I am having coffee by myself. Protein shakes now. The gal at the airport. She's fallen in love with my dog. Isn't that great?

She loves Ellie and Ellie lives there now. All the guys in the cargo office, they love Ellie! And there is always someone there so she is not lonely. She doesn't howl. I think. I don't hear her howl all the time anymore. Thank God. And that's good. That's very good.

BACK AT THE GYM

WENDY

HEY, Where you been?
The kid at the desk catcalls to me.
The seducer, he says,
"You look great!
How's your food?
You look great!
Give me twenty five!
You look great!
Must be that new man!"
I guess everyone can tell.
The horse show and the white truck
and the sleeping under the stars must have rubbed off on me!
Joe the Horse and
Lester the rancher
and …."it's all over you," he says.
"I'd like to get me a little taste of that!"

LIGHTS CHANGE. EDGES
APPEAR.

WENDY

I met this amazing man. Out of nowhere.
OK so I went online. Just to peek.
Nothing in common I was sure until I touched him.
Yes. I touched him. I had no choice!
We were sitting in his truck…his white pick up truck…
yes, I know! A white pick up truck.
We were sitting in his truck and
I did the same thing I did when I was 19.
I put my hand near the gear shift and there...
there it was, the brush,
I just wanted to find out if I would
still feel anything—
could feel anything.

We necked for what seemed hours in the truck.
We tried to touch all the parts of our bodies together.
I couldn't breathe so fucking greedy.
the gear shift, the gear shift in the way.
My skin drank the touch, my mouth, my lips.
Liquid everywhere dripping draining,
I couldn't stop touching him and he me.
even his denim jacket was on fire.
And like two teenagers we finally had to admit
that there was no bed to complete the operation.

The next morning he came back.
We found one….
"I'll go get a condom," he said.
I said to him. "I haven't had sex in …uh…forever and
I can't make babies anymore
This one's for us."
He laughed
And we fucked
And fucked
And fucked
Like drunk

Pussies meowing, stallions leaping
Maids a milking, knaves a licking
Dripping, drinking, breathing only now and then.

I grabbed onto that old man's body
and rode him bareback
for days, weeks months even!
Until we literally ripped the skin apart and
found ourselves really naked!
Every pore scrubbed clean and
every orifice exploded.

Fucking in the back of the truck under the stars
Fucking in fancy hotels and dives.
In New York City, in the country.
At the beach and in the mountains
With wringing hands and howling dogs
and it was still never enough…
And he would call my name and
we would hold on for dear LIFE!
Yes…… that's it LIFE.

I grabbed that man and we grabbed at life,
hands wide and fingers clawing.
Pouring life back and forth into each other
evening the scales
sloshing the excess
coating our toes.

I didn't want to die.

I was done with death
And he poured life and I poured life
and we couldn't stop.
we couldn't stop,
we couldn't stop.

And not once did I think of Evan.
I just thought of the red dragon India print
on my lovers bed.
And the way he kept my blue sarong
and flung it over the dragon
so that our scents never lost track of each other.
"Remember me," he said to me.
"Your body is your metaphor," he said to me.

One night we fucked so hard my bones rattled.
It was something in the way he held me down or
Let me up or wouldn't let me off the hook.
"Live goddammit!"
"Yes," I said. "Yes, oh yes."
I said yes.

"I'll never live with you, Wendy. I want you to know that.
And I met someone else and I'm going to follow that…"
I looked at my lover, his eyes wide, terrified.
He looked like a scared little doggie
who had lost the scent of lonely.
Ah-oooooo-oo.

It stopped then.
How do you thank your lover for your life
and the reintroduction to alone?
Lonely may hide in the shadow for awhile,
come and go at will.
But alone is the constant companion
always available for embrace.
How do you thank your lover for your life and
Learn to live without him?

                        SHE CROSSES AND FLOPS
                        BACK ON THE BED.

Fuck it! I will not move my legs

Except over someone's shoulders!
I prefer to make love.
I prefer to eat.
The dog ate my shoes.
I lost my homework!
I slept late!

                SHE YAWNS AND LAUGHS

The truth is, that
Alone can be friendly.
Alone can be a reminder of what
Was okay way before houses and husbands
And doggies and big love.

                SHE CROSSES TO CON-
                FRONT HER LOVER.

"I'm moving back to New York.
Gonna start again when it all began."
"Now don't be cheap with your new bed, Wendy.
Very important to have a good bed."
My lovers blessing on my next step.

So, I fly to the other coast to begin again
I find a sweet apartment in midtown.
I move in, unpack my things,
Set up my bed.
It's the same one.
I made it.
I'm lying in it.
It suits me just fine.

New York is a wonder!
I can't stay still!
People walk here and
They move…moving, moving!

I walk right down the street and there's Times Square.
And a few blocks that way is the park
And that way is the river.

I take the subway everywhere.
There are lots of stairs so
I step up! And I step up!
Definitely no elevator on 79th Street
on the number 1 line. I just came from there,
Zabars, and H and H..
But there is only one flight of stairs
Ten, twelve steps.
Many stations have two flights.

34th Street is supposed to have an elevator
at least there was a sign up there saying
it was going to be installed.
But I haven't seen it.
I think it will be on the other platform.
The 2 or 3 trains rather than the 1.
But the 1 train…. The local.
Is on the outside track. So, again only one flight
Of stairs is involved!
If you get out at 34th Street….

Ha! Who cares?
Evan is nowhere to be found.
He hates New York!

I brave the station at 53rd Street and 7th Avenue.
And I step up. I step up.
Twelve steps, fourteen, twenty five.
Another flight!
My knee is creaky,
But I am moving, moving,
Until I can't.
My knee is creaky.

My knee is gone!
Ow! I can't... Ow!

I find a gym and can't make it to the door
I find a doctor and he tells me no good news
I find a grocery delivery service and they tell me
They have a discount rate for disabled seniors.

I try to force a change
But I can do nothing
But sit, listen, wait, heal.
Dammit.
Well, at least I won't bump into the furniture.

> SHE IS STRANDED ON HER BED. SHE REACHES DOWN TO A PACKING BOX AND OPENS IT.

Oh my God. Evan's tee shirts!
I thought I left them back...

> SHE UNROLLS THEM AND LOOKS AT THE LEGENDS

Limahuli Gardens. Tom Cat Grill.

Toby's Feed Barn.
They're barely serving hay to horses there anymore
Across from the Bovine Bakery there on Main Street.
Can you imagine that, Evan?
Those morning buns in that beautiful town
So many summers and beaches and meals and fog.
Let's live there and grow old together. On the beach near Big
Sur. It's the only place we never fight!" you said to me.
It's where I spread your ashes.

> SHE MAKES A DECISION AND CROSSES TO THE COUNTER AND GETS THE SCISSORS.

I cut the fabric.
The incisions on your beautiful body.
There are no tubes hanging now.
No pain for you.
The scissor snugly places the fabric in its teeth.
It cuts clean and strong, no blood.

And Hog Island Oysters in grey,
The scissors in my hands.
And Hog Island Oysters in orange,
The blades in my mouth.
And Hog Island Oysters in blue
And my teeth on the fabric
I try to eat it.
The blade cuts clean and
The pieces are now even,
measured, balanced, digested.
Bits and pieces of then and now.
I make a quilt.

> SHE WRAPS THE QUILT ROUND HER AS SHE LIMPS TO THE ROCKING CHAIR CENTER.

I watch a lot of television while I heal.
My own girl man cave.
Evan used to turn the sound off.
He said he liked to watch the colors move.
I started that way, but it got too noisy.
So, I turned the sound on the other night.

It was a walk in the cemetery in Rome
Where Keats is buried and Shelley and Gregory Corso
And lots of others.
Overlooked by a huge pyramid built in 300 AD.
Or maybe before, time collapses after all.
The cemetery is full of angels and monuments
And layers and layers of regret.
The monuments insist that man is artifact.
He cannot die, he cannot transmute. And neither can we!
The dead must be as planted,
by those alive, as if still alive.
Is this the use of grief, to keep them in stone?
This cannot be what death truly is.. surely.
Or the life for those left behind!
No, no, no!

        HER MOOD BRIGHTENS!
        LIGHT BULB!

There is a celebration of sorts to be had!
Maybe it's Christmas, maybe it's spring.
It's a full moon and
I drink a cuppa cheer.
I pull down the last maraca from the music case
And I let myself sing.
"Or would you like to swing on a star."

The TV is quiet. The dead people are left stone
And above me is a moonlight that pierces
Right through it all.

I thrust myself against memory and
I pass right through it.
I am become memory.
And I sail on the disc of the moon
As it passes above me and
I am part of the moon!

I feel the slip and slide of
A ride against the sky..

"Wendy! Wendy! When you are sleeping in your silly bed, you might be sailing about with me, saying funny things to the stars!"

I sail through the night,
Laughing at the donkey moon
On a silver chord that lifts
Past Rome, past monuments and
Televisions and death and
Soaring in light,
And it's just fine because it is
WHAT IS!
We are all just WHAT IS!

Oh, I have spent so much time
Coming from then to now
As if there is such a thing as sequence.
It is all the same, silly fool.
We are here.
We are all here.
We are all here.
All the time.
Ha!

                                      LIGHTS CHANGE

It's spring and Sunday
And I am able to walk a bit now.
I practice my path, round the corner,
To the park, past the fruit stand.
And I look up
And I see him.
My husband, today.
Evan David Stuart as he was.

The cut of his smile finds me like a laser
applauding my progress.
Evan? Gone. He is breeze.

Just like they say.
A glimpse of then and now
As above, so below.
I experience thinness
The thinness of the membrane,
The barrier we just think is there.
And if I am honest,
I experience it all the time.
Evan, there.
As he was, as he is.
He shows himself
A gift.

I stop at the flower stand and
there are white lilies
Left here for me.
I know this.

On our honeymoon, Evan and I perch on
Our perfect Parisian balcony
And watch as a grey coated messenger comes toward us.
His hand is held high with a bunch of white lilies,
Floating over the heads of the bustling passers by.
And those lilies climb the stairs and
Come into our bridal chamber and
They open and fill the room with the sweetest scent.
I think I will choke on such a well of sweetness.
There is no other way but to be so deeply present in
This moment of marriage.
The joining of the past into the very present of now.

And I have this gift of white lilies.
Now, time past time

I have the lilies and sit through the night
I am a companion to the flowers
I put my hand out to touch them.
But I needn't. They are there if I touch them or not.
Time collapses and love remains as beauty through time.
I live life as I am.
Simple, loved, loving, alone.
Surely we must trust past pain
That beauty will out again and again
In the mysterious cycle
Of endless simplicity.

END OF PLAY

Actress, writer, producer and educator Susan Merson (www.susanmerson.com) started her New York acting career on Broadway in Zeffirelli's SATURDAY SUNDAY MONDAY, and then most notably as part of the original company of VANITIES. Moving to Los Angeles she expanded her acting resume to include most major television dramas and several feature films. She has written and performed nine solo shows and her book YOUR NAME HERE; AN ACTRESS WRITERS GUIDE TO SOLO PERFORMANCE remains a popular seller on Amazon, along with her novel, DREAMING IN DAYLIGHT. Her plays have been performed across the country including the plays in this volume in addition to the noted BOUNTY OF LACE and WHITE BIRCHES included in recent anthologies.Long time moderator of the LA WRITERS BLOC, she continues to mentor writers and actors in both New York and Los Angeles. She currently teaches Playwrighting at California State University/ Fullerton and serves as the Founder and Producing Artistic Director of NEW YORK THEATRE INTENSIVES (www.nytheatreintensives.org)

Also by Susan Merson

Your Name Here:
A Writer/Actor's Guide to Solo Performance
by Susan Merson
Theater/Acting
ISBN: 1-932993-03-7
$17.96 USD/ 168 pages

An essential bare bones guide to getting your own solo play into the world!

For actors, writers and public speakers of all kinds.

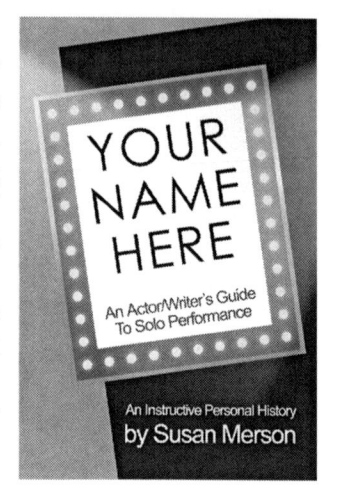

Dreaming in Daylight
by Susan Merson
Adult Literary Fiction
ISBN: 978-1-932993-97-4
$17.95 USD / 280 pages
From [blocpress]
a Star Publish LLC Imprint

Rose Shiner's father Leo, a one time carnival barker and opera producer, prefers Puccini's world to his own. Belle, Rose's mother, fights debilitating depression, desperate to step up from her youth on the Canadian prairie to a suburban castle. Rosie struggles mightily to grow in this shadow world, fighting through nightmares to find dreams steady and safe enough to sustain her in daylight.